THE SPIRITUAL MESSAGE
OF
MODERN ENGLISH POETRY

THE SPIRITUAL MESSAGE
OF
MODERN ENGLISH POETRY

86503

BY
ARTHUR S. HOYT

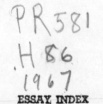

Essay Index Reprint Series

BOOKS FOR LIBRARIES PRESS, INC.
FREEPORT, NEW YORK

First published 1924
Reprinted 1967

To

HILDEGARDE HOYT SWIFT

AND

ARTHUR LESSNER SWIFT, Jr.

KEEN AND APPRECIATIVE CRITICS OF
THEIR FATHER'S WORK, THIS BOOK
IS AFFECTIONATELY DEDICATED

FOREWORD

THIS is not a venture in literary criticism. It would be foolish to venture where so many great ones have trod. The book is just what the title suggests, the effort to show the relation of modern English poetry to the higher thought and impulse of the race.

The author is largely indebted to others. The thoughts of many minds will doubtless be found in these pages, the result of life-long study and teaching.

Special mention, however, should be made of such books as Stopford Brooke's Tennyson and Browning, Sir Henry Jones and Dr. John A. Hutton on Browning, Henry van Dyke's Tennyson, the Introductions to In Memoriam by Davidson and Genung, Miss Vida Scudder's studies in both the spiritual and social message of modern English Literature, and Chapman's "English Literature, in Account with Religion."

The very idea that poetry has a message may be distasteful to some critics. What end can there be beyond poetry itself? But as life is full of meaning, constant witness to the spirit's striving after the Eternal, poetry as the most subtle and penetrative interpretation of life, must bring its testimony. Religion can not express itself without poetry, and the noblest poetry has been religious.

And no men need poetry more than the teachers of religion. The highest truths of religion can not be conceived without imagination, and they can not be made realities to the common mind without its pictures of ethereal hue. Imagination first declines, and when the vision splendid is lost, the sermon sinks to a wearisome and lifeless dogma.

And there is good thought and inspiration in the poets as nowhere else. Here the soul can slake its thirst and renew its strength.

In an age when so many of its thinkers are marked by a cynical pessimism, the spiritual teacher can take good heart at the growing light of poetry. We shall not rejoice in this light, if we look too closely within churchly confines. The spirit of God is as broad as human need and human effort.

> "And not by eastern windows only,
>   When daylight comes, comes in the light,
> In front the sun climbs slow, how slowly,
>   But westward, look, the land is bright."

Is there to be a new day for faith? Is the growing knowledge to be crowned by a growing reverence and charity? What so prophetic as the modern poet? Listen to the voice of John Drinkwater who sings in the growing dawn——

> "O heart, be ready now,
>   Cold in your night, be ready now to sing—
> Dawn as it wakes the sleeping bird on bough,
>   Shall summon you to instant reckoning,—
> She is your dawn, O heart,—
>   Sing till the night of death shall come, the
>   gospel of her light."

August, 1923.

CONTENTS

CHAPTER I

Creative Forces

THE SPIRITUAL MESSAGE OF MODERN ENGLISH POETRY

CHAPTER I

CREATIVE FORCES

There are two aspects or ideas of poetry, the *artistic* and *prophetic*. They are not often kept consciously distinct, but as one or the other prevails, poetry becomes *critical* or *creative*. Both express a truth of poetry. Writing is not poetry that is devoid of invention and harmony, that has no music in its numbers, no beauty in its images. "Poetry in its complete sympathy with beauty," says Leigh Hunt, "must of necessity leave no sense of the beautiful, and no power over its forms unmanifested." But in poetry as in every other expression of life, the form is often dwelt upon at the expense of the spirit. The forces of the soul are spent upon refining and not upon finding, and poetry becomes critical, polite and formal, the luxury of a few, a sort of "lordly pleasure-house," and not the foregleam and foreword of progress, the energy of social and spiritual recreation.

The lower view, and I am sorry to say the too common view, of poetry is voiced by Pope the master of the critical school: "Poetry and criticism are by no means the universal concern of the world, but only the affair of idle men who write in their closets, and of idle men who read there. All the advantages I can think of, accruing from a genius for poetry, are the agreeable power of self-amusement, when a man is idle or alone, the privilege of being admitted into the best company, and the freedom of saying as many careless things as other people without being so severely remarked on." This perhaps is the lowest depth of the mere artistic view of poetry—pleasers of self.

But such a view is far below the true definition of poetry and the conception which the great poets have had of their work. The prophetic view has the largest truth in it. We must regard the *interpretative* power of the noblest poetry, revealing and representing the directive and creative thoughts of men, and touching the profound feelings that make the impulses of human action. The imagination is the noblest power of vision. It flashes its way where reason painfully gropes. By its reaches the otherwise independent and unrelated facts of the natural world are bound into order and movement, and by its aid the thoughts of God are recorded for human eyes. The missing link has never been found; it is imagination that bridges the gulf and thinks of the universe and life as continuous creation. And the sensitiveness of the poet, the cords of feeling that vibrate to the faintest breath of life, thrill with the unexpressed instincts and yearnings of the heart, grasp relations and facts larger and truer than in common hours, "a more ample greatness, a more exact goodness, a more absolute variety," and body forth the dim and intangible visions that at times haunt all men.

Every definition of poetry that is felt to be at all true to its deeper meaning tries to express the prophetic element. "Poetry is a criticism of life." "Poetry speaks out the thought that lies in things." "Poetry is the presentment in musical form to the imagination of noble grounds for the noble emotions."

And the great poets themselves have often felt that they were voices of a higher wisdom, that "poetry hath some participation of divineness." The best minds have always held poetry to be in some sort a revelation, and the critics are not so very wrong in sometimes seeing more in great poems than the poets themselves were conscious of writing. Milton, writing of the conditions under which poetry is possible, says: "This is not to be obtained but by devout prayer to that Eternal Spirit that can enrich with all utterance and knowledge, and sends his Seraphim with the hallowed fire of his altar, to touch and purify the lips of whom He pleases." Even a child of nature like Robert Burns felt that he was a dedicated spirit. The muse of Scotch poetry, the genius of native land, appears to him and gives him his commission:

> I saw thee seek the sounding shore,
> Delighted with the dashing roar;
> Or when the North his fleecy store
>   Drove through the sky,—
> I saw grim nature's visage hoar
>   Struck thy young eye.

> Or when the deep, green-mantled earth,
> Warm cherished ev'ry flow'ret's birth,
> And joy and music pouring forth
>   In every grove—
> I saw thee eye the gen'ral mirth
>   With boundless love.

"Poet and prophet differ greatly in our loose modern notions of them," says Carlyle. "In some old languages the titles are synonymous: *vates* means both Prophet and Poet: and indeed at all times Prophet and Poet, well understood, have much kindred meaning. Fundamentally indeed they are still the same; in this most important respect especially, that they have penetrated both of them into the sacred mystery of the universe. Whoever may forget this divine mystery, as the realized thought of God, the *vates*, whether Prophet or Poet, has penetrated into it, is a man sent hither to make it more impressively known to us."

Tennyson has clearly expressed his thought of the Poet's calling—

The Poet in a golden clime was born,
　With golden stars above;
Dower'd with the hate of hate, the scorn of scorn,
　The love of love.

He saw through life and death, through good and ill,
　He saw through his own soul;
The marvel of the everlasting will,
　An open scroll,
　Before him lay.

Then truth was multiplied on truth: the world
　Like one great garden show'd,
And through the wreaths of floating dark upcurled
　Rare sunrise flow'd.

And freedom rear'd in that august sunrise,
　Her beautiful, bold brow,
When rites and forms before his burning eyes
　Melted like snow.

Rare gifts of nature, the eye that reads the everlasting will, the apostleship of light, truth, liberty, the power to see the life and meaning beneath all forms,—such a man is verily sent of God.

Both Robert Browning and Mrs. Browning believed that poetry is, in the inception, an inspiration. "The more one sits and thinks over the creative process," says Robert Browning in the recently published letters, "the more it confirms itself an inspiration, nothing more or less."

I do not mean to suggest that there is no difference between the inspiration of the noblest poetry and that of the writers of the Bible. But the difference lies in the purpose of each more than in anything else. The inspiration of the Bible is to give the historic revelation of Christianity; the inspiration of the noblest poetry is to interpret the facts of daily experience. They are in some sense complement and correlate of each other. As the Bible has been the food for the loftiest imagination, as its most spiritual truths make their appeal through imagination and feeling,— cannot be understood without the poetic capacity, and often find their only suitable expression in the form of poetry itself—; so poetry sustains the faculty of faith, casts over the common things of life an ideal light, pierces the veil of sense and reads the spiritual truths of man and the universe, is a witness for God and the spirit and immortality. It is not wrong to connect Mr. Darwin's loss of interest in Christianity with his waning love for poetry.

So an interpretation of the poets has its place in the studies of religion. Poetry belongs to polite learning (though one may dislike the word "polite"),—the necessary culture of a mind that loves truth and beauty, the training of the necessary faculties of the spiritual life, imagination and emotion.   But more than this: the great poets are voices to the soul.   Dante and Goethe, Shakspere and Milton, Wordsworth and Tennyson and Browning are prophets of the spiritual life as truly as Augustine and Luther and Calvin and Wesley and Newman.   In a recent series of studies of great devotional helps, "In Memoriam," "Saul," and "Rabbi Ben Ezra" were rightly put with "Pilgrim's Progress" and "Holy Living and Dying."   We have

> the animating faith,
> That poets even as prophets,
> Have each his own peculiar faculty,
> Heaven's gift, a sense that fits them to perceive
> Objects unseen before.

The Poet-Prophets are the subtle interpreters of their time; they speak upon the house-top what is whispered in the ear: they voice the dim and intangible yearnings and visions of the many.   And so they are not only the resultant expression of the generation, the word of the age-consciousness; but they mark the way of thought and life, become leaders, creators, of social and spiritual progress.   But the man and his age are to be interpreted together.   "No man," says Mr. Froude, "in single contact with the facts of his own time, could produce a Pallas, a Madonna, a King Lear.   Such works are the result of a nation's spirit." And to interpret aright the higher message of modern English poetry, we must feel the forces it voiced and thereby helped to their dominance.

What in modern life has been creative?   What have been the forces of the higher life of the last hundred years?   They have been a new view of nature, a new interest in man, a new spirit as to the problems of being: scientific, democratic, religious. These are the forces that have profoundly stirred the hearts of men, made the last century creative, and lifted up its chosen souls as seers and singers.

The strongest single force of the century has been the scientific movement. Many of the sciences had been formed before: men had been observing the phenomena of nature and these were slowly modifying their ideas of the universe and of man; but not until the nineteenth century did the scientific habit become the ruling spirit, and a philosophy was formed of the facts observed that made essentially a new view of nature. It is the theory of *Development*. No doubt the idea of growth, of orderly progress, was long in the minds of men. It was as truly in the air as the thought of a new world before Columbus set sail from Palos. There were many hints and suggestions before Darwin gave it strict statement in Science and Spencer in Philosophy.

Miss Scudder, in "The Life of the Spirit in the Modern English Poets," says that "the chief poetic passages which treat directly the modern evolutionary conception are really prophetic, written before the new creed was fairly spoken. There are three great modern passages dealing with the universe as a whole in relation to man: the second and fourth acts of Shelley's 'Prometheus Unbound,' written in 1819; the lines in the last act of Browning's 'Paracelsus,' written in 1833; and parts of Tennyson's 'In Memoriam,' published in 1850. 'The Origin of Species' was not published till 1859; yet every one of these passages expresses a clear conception of evolution as distinct from the then current idea of spasmodic and special creations." It may not be easy to find the truth in Shelley's bewildering dream of an unconscious universe gradually informed with conscious life and love: but Browning's lines leave no doubt as to his conception of an evolution controlled and filled by God:

> The center-fire heaves underneath the earth,
> And the earth changes like a human face.
>   Thus God dwells in all,
> From life's minute beginnings, up at last
> To man, the consummation of this scheme
> Of being, the completion of this sphere
> Of life.

And more wonderful still is the prophecy of Tennyson in "In Memoriam,"—after the years of question and reflection still the poetic interpretation of development. It is the 118th song:

>   They say,
> The solid earth whereon we tread
>
> In tracts of fluent heat began,
>   And grew to seeming-random forms,
>   The seeming prey of cyclic storms,
> Till at the last arose the man;
>
> Who throve and branch'd from clime to clime,
>   The herald of a higher race,
>   And of himself in higher place,
> If so he type this work of time
>
> Within himself, from more to more;
>   Or, crown'd with attributes of woe
>   Like glories, move his course, and show
> That life is not as idle ore,

But iron dug from central gloom,
  And heated hot with burning fears,
  And dipt in baths of hissing tears,
And batter'd with the shocks of doom

To shape and use.   Arise and fly
  The reeling Faun, the sensual feast;
  Move upward, working out the beast,
And let the ape and tiger die.

But has the scientific movement enriched the thought of men and given poetry a new inspiration? It does not seem to be the first effect of scientific study; and it is thought by many to be materialistic rather than spiritual, to lessen ideality by the removal of mystery, to clip the wings of imagination by its reverence for fact and law. Wordsworth voices the fear and the scorn of the worldly spirit that puts us out of tune with the true music of nature:

  Great God! I'd rather be
A pagan suckled in a creed outworn;
So might I, standing on this pleasant lea,
Have glimpses that would make me less forlorn;
Have sight of Proteus rising from the sea;
Or hear old Triton blow his wreathed horn.

But Wordsworth loved truth too well to fear the unveiling of science; he knew nature too well to fear that the study of man could do less than increase the wonder and divineness of being. He saw the richer field of imagination through the labors of men. "The man of science seeks truth as a remote and unknown benefactor; he cherishes and loves it in his solitude. The poet, singing a song in which all human beings join with him, rejoices in the presence of truth as our visible friend and hourly companion. Poetry is the breath and finer spirit of all knowledge; it is the impassioned expression which is on the countenance of science. If the labors of the men of science should ever create any material revolution, direct or indirect, in our condition, and in the impressions which we habitually receive, the poet will sleep then no more than at present; he will be ready to follow the steps of the man of science, not only in these general indirect effects, but he will be at his side, carrying sensation into the midst of the objects of science itself. . . . If the time should ever come when what is now called science, thus familiarized to men, shall be ready to put on as it were a form of flesh and blood, the poet will lend his divine spirit to aid the transfiguration, and will welcome the Being thus produced as a dear and genuine inmate of the household of man."

The faith of Wordsworth has been richly justified by the results of scientific thought already. Whatever widens the realm of knowledge widens the realm of imagination. Not only has the poet stood beside the scientist and carried *"sensation* into the midst of the objects of science," as already intimated, *felt* the truth after which others were painfully groping; but scientific thought has given powerful impulse to literature.

The idea of force at the heart of things, ever at work changing and shaping, the dynamic of *endless growth*, has given a new interest to nature. It is not finished, fixed, mechanical; but a living thing with the endless changes of motion, and the mysterious charm of an ever-becoming and unfolding purpose. The imagination of the poets has kept them from the too common mistake of the scientists of making force impersonal, and they have felt a mighty Being awake and watched the ongoings of his life. So nature is an object of study and feeling as never before. Not the mere background of man's life, but the environment, the garden, the home, and almost the heaven. There is little love of nature in the older literature as we now know it. It is said that there is hardly a new symbol of nature in the poets from Shakspere to Burns. But the idea of the restless and creative force at the heart of things has given interest to the minutest phases, the most transient changes of natural life. So a world of new imagery has been found to express the unfolding revelation. It is the symbolism of life, of changing, growing life.

The earth changes like a human face.

And a new feeling for nature has come in the view of force as growth. There is a joy in living, in feeling one's self a part of this boundless life, in receiving the impulses of this boundless energy. Not melancholy but *hope* is the message of the green earth and the rolling year. Not the passing glory, the fading flower, the falling leaf, but the mutability of earth,— as the conservation of life, the imperishableness of all good, one passing only to give place to a higher life. The idea of inner force that gives growth to natural things has not only given new and brighter aspects to nature, but has led to the view of human life as development. So there is a new treatment of character in literature. We are not so interested in external facts, in actions, however thrilling the story of them may be,—as in the inner life, the motives and passions, the contest within, soul at war with sense, the action of inherited tendencies on environment, the processes of soul-growth, the shaping of human destiny. The greatest masters of the old romance cannot hold the page to the novelist to-day of motive and purpose, who makes us conscious of the profound forces of human life. Jane Austen may be a greater artist than Margaret Deland, but she lives in a provincial world compared with the modern. In fact modern literature is the drama of the inner life. Even the poetry of reflection, the analysis of thought itself apart from the fascination of action, has a new vitality from this principle of growth, as you will see by comparing Arnold and Clough, Tennyson and Browning in their most subjective moods, with the dead, didactic verse of the eighteenth century.

The scientific spirit has given us a universe tremulous with charm, life tragic with import. "The passion for development controls our writers. Ours is the age of the poetry of struggle, not of victory; of desire, not of achievement; of growth, not of rest."

And with this sense of growth, is a striving after *unity*, a feeling at heart that all must be connected with an infinite reason, and working out a single purpose which the infinite mind sees. Fragments of force, disconnected events, purposeless efforts, these are intolerable to the deeper thought of life. The idea of unity connects human life with the universe; we rise out of the lower life and are now strangely connected with it. Underneath our feet are cosmic fires, across our sky sweep cosmic winds, and within our very being are moving forces connecting us with the very beginnings of life, and suggesting their prophecy of what we may be.

We are bound up with human lives everywhere.

The larger, truer man is ever before our eyes. The problem of the individual is the problem of society.

The sense of the larger unity of life brought by the scientific movement manifests itself in the spirit of literature and in the details of its work. Every work must have a worthy reason for being. Even our nonsense must have logic and purpose. Many strange and popular conceits of the older writers are simply stupid to the modern mind. You can hardly conceive of a gifted mind to-day spending its art upon a theme without dignity or lofty aspiration, like Pope's "Rape of the Lock."

There is a passion for *fact*, the facts of the outer and the inner world. The impossible is ruled out. Of course the danger of this scientific spirit in literature is in the lower realism, the photographic view of life, picturing just what we see. The difference here will depend upon the organ of vision. It may see with the eyes of a Zola or an Ian Maclaren. But even Zola is not all flesh: he can read the soul in the condemned Dreyfus, and show his own soul in the heroic plea for the wronged. The fact is the truest idealism rises from the realistic basis, and this the scientific spirit has brought into literature. Men and women are better than gnomes and ghosts and impossible knights-errant.

There is a marvelous feeling for detail in modern verse, that comes from this passion for fact, this desire for reality, the sense of the worth because the vital relation of every fact of life. So on every hand are new subjects for poetry, a vastly widened field, as wide as the realms of modern thought, and made fit subjects for poetry, lifted into the realm of the imagination, by the great principles of life, its growth and unity. Poetry lends its divine inspiration to give this great body of facts the semblance of flesh and blood, to infuse into it *the breath of life.*

A second influence that has mightily touched modern English poetry, found voice in its best pages, and in turn gained its noblest impulse from the poets, has been the *Democratic movement.*

All truly great poets are universal in their sympathies and touch truths that bring out the essential nature of man; and in this way by cutting through the accidental and factitious to the essential, they give men common hopes and common sympathies. *Dante,* a Romanist, places men under one moral government rather than under the laws of the Church. *Milton* broke from his natural association of Church and Royalist, to espouse the cause of the people in the Puritan Revolution. In *Cowper,* through his religious feelings, the idea of mankind as a whole is first seen in English song. His interest in man is as wide as the world. He is profoundly moved by all the social and moral questions of the race. He deals with life as a sublime reality. *Burns* gave even a stronger impulse to the democratic spirit. All the interests of man touched his heart. He felt keenly and sang passionately and musically of all that entered into the homely experiences of life about him. *Byron* and *Shelley,* born aristocrats, were not defenders of class and hereditary privilege, but made song the weapon of human rights.

The new idea of man, thus voiced by the poets, had been developing for a century under the purer teaching of Christianity as in the Wesley revival in England, in the reaction from a false view of state and Church under the radical thinkers of France, and in the ever-growing freedom and reach of commerce and travel.

The American Revolution gave force and movement to the cause of human rights. The impassioned words of orators on both sides of the sea quickened the popular thought. Natural rights belonged to every man and bound all men together. There was the society of man, wider and more important than the narrow sets of kindred and taste. There was the state of man, in which each man had the sovereignty of a citizen. So wealth, class, customs, powers of state, whatever interfered with the possession and use of natural rights, must be overthrown as hostile to the true interests of man. Such ideas had long been expressed by French writers: they were expressed in action by the overthrow of the Bastile in 1789, and in the proclamation of the new constitution in the following year. They at once became living powers in the world. Wordsworth, Coleridge, Southey, accepted them at first, but refused to follow them into the violence of the Reign of Terror. *Scott* was driven to the romantic past by his pain at the present. *Byron* absorbed their spirit and expressed it in his rebellion against social and moral laws. When these ideas had lost their force, *Shelley* reëxpressed them in more ideal form.

The effect upon literature of the popular ideas concerning the rights of man, was to increase the resistance to the bondage of criticism, and by the powerful feelings they kindled in men, to bring passion into style in its work about man and nature. The movements for civil liberty entered as strongly into the poetry of the century, as the Protestant Reformation, the movement of religious liberty, affected the literature of the sixteenth and seventeenth centuries, the poetry of Spenser and Shakspere and Milton.

A *third* force of the higher life of the century has been philosophic and religious, a new spirit as to the questions of being. Every question of nature must in the end be a question of man. And every question of human rights suggests the problem of the soul from which these rights arise.

The influences in philosophy and religion have been vigorous and progressive. It has been a struggle of conflicting theories.

The utilitarian tendency of English thought was further developed by James Mill and Jeremy Bentham. The critical and skeptical tendencies of the utilitarian school called forth a line of Scotch metaphysicians, Reid and Hamilton and their followers, the school of natural realists, the strong supporters of the spiritual life.

The latent materialism of Locke, in his quiet denial of innate ideas, had sprung up in the quicker soil of France into religious unbelief and revolutionary social theories. And this reflex wave of English philosophy, returning through the French mind, made the contest the more intense.

Coleridge, an eager student of all these enquiries, interpreted to English minds the transcendental thought of Germany, and gave emphasis to the facts of our higher, intuitive nature.

The new religious zeal of the age, striving for the neglected at home and abroad, held firmly through all speculation and attack to the central truths of Christianity and discovered new lines of intellectual defense. "Thus the nineteenth century opened a pregnant spring-time, in which the useful, the beautiful, and the worthless struggled together for sunlight."

Through the century science, philosophy, theology

have been in ceaseless action and reaction. The earlier schools have been modified by evolutionary philosophy and new forms of idealism. Revolt has softened into agnosticism. The critical spirit has grown to be the questioning one,

> That will not make its judgments blind.

There is a fearless, earnest, and on the whole reverent spirit of enquiry. The questions of the soul are felt to be the supreme questions of life.

These age-forces, of science, democracy, religion, are all creative. They have fed the imagination and stirred the emotions and helped to produce an age of great poetry.

Of the remarkable group of singers in the first third of the century, Scott, Coleridge, Southey, Byron, Shelley, Keats, Wordsworth, I take the last as the best embodiment of the spirit of the times, as the one in whom we understand its temper and feel its directive force. As Matthew Arnold says, comparing Wordsworth with contemporary poets, "He deals with more life than they do: he deals with life as a whole more powerfully." Such a life must have a message for the soul of man.

CHAPTER II

The Poet of the Hills

CHAPTER II

THE POET OF THE HILLS

Fifty years ago Wordsworth was a prophet to the best minds of the English race. Scores of men who have quickened our minds and given us purified taste, like Arnold and Kingsley, Robertson and Stanley, Shairp and Bryant and Lowell were glad to say of Wordsworth, transferring what the poet writes of his sister,—

> He gave me eyes, he gave me ears,
> And humble cares, and delicate fears;
> A heart the fountain of sweet tears,
> And love and thought and joy.

The other day a follower of Izaak Walton was wading waist-deep in the waters of an Adirondack stream. The river had swept with a rapid and shallow curve into a long, quiet and pebbly pool, bordered with alders and partly shaded with the beeches and spruces of a virgin forest. The day's fishing must come to an end for the lower rim of the sun was beginning to touch the western tree line, and a trail of three miles led over the hills to the camp. A single cast more where the current ripples under the overhanging bank. A big trout rises to the tail-fly and comes a little short. He breaks water at a second cast and is struck hard and the contest for the creel begins. But the fish is lightly hooked and the strong deep current is against the angler and a few minutes' struggle gives the big fish his freedom again. A swarm of black flies settle upon the fisherman and add their mocking comment to the day's unlucky ending. When from the thicket on the north bank a chorus of wood-thrushes begin their vesper song. "No human voice, no instrument that human skill has devised, can give that almost holy quality of tone. It was song, the rapturous outpouring of the heart; and it was worship, lifting the soul out of every hindering vestment to thrill with the thoughts of God." How was it that the whole scene was clothed in new light, that the earth seemed to have a new beauty and welcome for her child, that this wondrous frame of things was instinct with divine life. It was Wordsworth who had helped to make the soul sensitive to the impress of higher powers, who had given "an eye made quiet by the power of harmony, and the deep power of joy, to see into the life of things." And it is well at times to be called away from the dust and din of city streets, away from the close air of artificial life, away from the strife of tongues, to live in the sun and feel how good it is, to know how few are the wants of man, to find life like an October morning transparent to the very verge, to wake truths that perish never.

Wordsworth is called the poet of the hills. Only the mountains could make him what he was. The creative and inspiring soul is above every circumstance and Wordsworth would have been Wordsworth anywhere, but God placed him in an environment that called forth the impulses of deepest birth. His poetry has not only the unity of great ideas, but the unity of a single background. He spent his whole life almost within sight of Skiddaw and Helvellyn. As John Ruskin found strange delight in getting a land-line cutting against the sky and traced his power to judge of art from gazing at the Cumberland hillsides or the long lines of surf, so Wordsworth felt the passion of the haunting cataract, in the solitude of the hills found the grandeur of man's nature, and in the visions of the upper air had awakened

> those shadowy recollections,
> Which be they what they may,
> Are yet the fountain light of all our day,
> Are yet a master light of all our seeing.

Wordsworth spent his youth among the hills. He never knew the leveling and commonizing influence of crowded centers, life limited and suppressed by the stereotyping of form. He grew as naturally and as freely as a tree of the field. He grew by all those indefinable influences of field and forest, lake and mountain, the cosmic forces that made him a child of Nature. What other child has been so early and deeply moved by the scenes and forces of the natural world! He was in love with its color, its motion, its changing expression; Nature was a satisfying companionship. She was food, playmate, nurse, mother. Have we any words in literature to be put beside those of Wordsworth in "Tintern Abbey" as the truthful portrait of a similar boyhood:

> The sounding cataract
> Haunted me like a passion: the tall rock,
> The mountain, and the deep and gloomy wood,
> Their colors and their forms, were then to me

An appetite: a feeling and a love,
That had no need of a remoter charm,
By thought supplied, or any interest
Unborrowed from the eye.

And later when his dreams of brotherhood were shattered by the excesses of the French Revolution, when he abandoned all moral questions in despair, and his eyes were closed to the visions of the hills, and his poetic power had gone with the closing of the spiritual eye, when the Philistines of doubt had made him a blind Samson shorn of his strength; then the "homely nurse" of his childhood restored him to his true self, the heated nature was calmed amid the scenes of his youth, the imagination regained its vigor and the heart was opened to the messages of the world. And through this deep experience of sorrow and meditation grew the power of spiritual interpretation, so that the senses were not a veil but an eye into the heart of things. The Poet stood now in a larger world. "His eye now looked on nature with the wonder of the world's childhood, mellowed with the reflective-ness of its mature age." Nature was more than a delicious sensation, an inspiring rapture: it was a profound revelation. The lover had become the seer.

And Wordsworth lived out of doors and composed out of doors and his best poems have the tonic of the mountain air. Dove Cottage and Allanbank and Rydal Mount were only shelters for the person; his real home was walled by the hills and the sky. "This is the place where he keeps his books," said the servant to the visitor at Rydal Mount, "his study is out of doors."

But who is he, with modest looks,
And clad in homely russet-brown?
He murmurs near the running brooks
A music sweeter than their own.

He is retired as noon-tide dew,
Or fountain in a noon-day grove;
And you must love him, ere to you
He will seem worthy of your love.

Wordsworth never had to say to himself, "Now I will study nature. Now I will see what secrets this world will yield to the inquisitive spirit." It was not so much a matter of study as of fellowship. It was the interpretation of a kindred feeling. He saw and felt because he loved.

The eye—it can not choose but see:
We cannot bid the ear be still;
Our bodies feel, where'er they be,
    Against, or with our will.

Nor less I deem that there are Powers
Which of themselves our minds impress;
That we can feed this mind of ours
    In a wise passiveness.

Think you, 'mid all this mighty sum
Of things forever speaking,
That nothing of itself will come
    But we must still be seeking?

Why did Wordsworth so love nature that he spent a life in receiving her impressions, that he found a satisfying companionship in her presences, that the meanest flower that blows could suggest thoughts too

deep for tears? Was it because of his rare endowment of imagination and feeling, that he saw more
minutely and felt more exquisitely than others the
manifold phases of the physical world; that form and
color and motion, order and harmony and beauty made
their appeal to his esthetic nature, that he was enrap-
tured of the music of the spheres? Not on esthetic
but on spiritual grounds is this to be accounted for.
It is only to be explained by his finding the spirit
within the form, and communing with the Infinite Life.
He received the impress not only of external form but
of those imperishable truths of being of which nature
is but the visible vesture.

Two truths underlie the world's highest poetry, viz.:
this world but the vestibule of the eternal, and God in
whom man lives hère and shall live forever. If imagination is a divine faculty, a power of vision, and grant
the existence of a spiritual world, a Great Spirit the
giver and Lord,—and poets, if their eyes are not
blinded by a false love, if imagination is kept true by
a pure love, must help the world to realize the highest
truths of being; they must be witnesses for God and
the soul and immortality. And they have been such
witnesses. Poets see and feel

> the ever-during power,
> And central peace subsisting at the heart
> Of endless agitation.

God presses on the spirit of the poet: in the hours when
that spirit aspires highest and acts noblest, this vast
appearance of things material is suddenly touched and
spiritualized. So the poets help to restore to us the
clearness of sight, and the vigor of faith,—the restoration of our truest selves.

Every reader of Wordsworth feels that there is something higher than his own life, something infinitely more than the impressions of material things upon his own mind, that he stands before visions of the hills, presences in the sky. Such poetry conduces to the sense of mystery; it helps to the feelings of awe and reverence; it leads at least into the vestibule of the temple. But does it carry us further, into the inner shrine, to kneel before the altar in gratitude and penitence and aspiration before the Father of our Spirits, the personal God of moral majesty and eternal compassion? Is the poetry of Wordsworth *Theistic?* Does he make us feel God clothing Himself in the light and beauty, and the form and force of nature?

There are those who think Wordsworth simply Pantheistic, that nature strikes the harp of life, and in its music the personal life of God and even self seem to tremble out of sight. And they think of such lines as the twenty-seventh sonnet:

> Listen! the mighty Being is awake,
> And doth with his eternal motion make
> A sound like thunder, everlastingly,

in which God and nature seem to be identified. Again in the poem to the daisy, he speaks of the influence of the lowly flower upon his own spirit, as something spiritual, but he does not go so far as to connect it with the message of the Eternal Spirit. Nature is spiritualized but not with the breath of the personal spirit:

> Fresh smitten by the morning ray
> When thou art up, alert and gay,
> Then, cheerful flower! my spirits play
>   With kindred gladness:

And when, at dusk, by dews opprest
Thou sink'st, the image of thy rest
Hath often eased my pensive breast
    Of careful sadness.

And all day long I number yet,
All seasons thro', another debt,
Which I, wherever thou art met,
    To thee am owing:

An instinct call it, a blind sense,
A happy, genial influence,
Coming one knows not how, nor whence,
    Nor whither going.

And in the short lyric, "A slumber did my spirit seal,"
the poet ends with the life returning to its mother
earth.

A slumber did my spirit seal;
    I had no human fears:
She seemed a thing that could not feel
    The touch of earthly years.

No motion has she now, no force:
    She neither hears nor sees,
Rolled round in earth's diurnal course,
    With rocks, and stones, and trees.

And so careless readers (not real students and lovers)
have sometimes thought that however loyal Wordsworth might be to the Church, it was more out of
respect to its social authority than to its spiritual, and
that in his real life he was simply a worshiper of
nature, using religious terms and full of religious feel-

ings, but meaning little more than the mysterious and awesome force or forces of the life of the world.

Now it is not claimed that Wordsworth ever set himself the distinct task of teaching Theism—at least not in his best poetry,—the formal, didactic spirit is not the poetic; but the lover of Wordsworth as firmly believes that he brings us into living touch with God, spiritual apprehension of Him, as that Nature herself is a revelation, that the "invisible things of Him are clearly seen by the things that are made."

Let us try to follow Wordsworth's own way of revealing God, not didactic teaching about God, but helping us to see and feel Him; perhaps it might be better to say God's way of training the poet into spiritual knowledge.

Wordsworth feels the *infinitude of life* around him and beyond him. That's the way a man comes to true self-knowledge and to spiritual desire, by feeling his own limitation, his weakness and littleness and ignorance in the face of forces that he cannot measure and thought that leads along too dizzy heights for him to follow. The immeasurableness and mystery of the world in which he lived possessed his imagination from a child and are strongly felt in his first poems. He felt it in the "disappearing line" of the public highway,

> that crossed
> The naked summit of a far-off hill,
> Beyond the limits that my feet had trod
> Was like an invitation into space,
> Boundless, or guide into eternity.

He felt it as he stood under the quiet stars, or as the night blackened with a coming storm; he drank in the

visionary power, he felt the moods of shadowy exalta-
tion, he retained the sense of possible sublimity. The
poem on "The Simplon Pass" expresses the infinite
environment of man's life.

> The immeasurable height
> Of woods decaying, never to be decayed,
> The stationary blasts of waterfalls,
> And in the narrow rent, at every turn,
> Winds thwarting winds bewildered and forlorn,
> Remained, no pleasant images of trees,
> Of sea or sky, no colors of green fields;
> But huge and mighty forms, that do not live
> Like living men, moved slowly through the mind
> By day, and were a trouble to my dreams.

After the "merciless ravage" of the hazel bushes,
he felt a sense of pain when he beheld the silent trees
and the intruding sky as though he had done despite to
a sentient life:

> Then, dearest maiden! move along these shades
> In gentleness of heart; with gentle hand
> Touch—for there is a spirit in the woods.

and in "Expostulation and Reply" he voices the sense
of Powers

> Which of themselves our minds impress.

This feeling of mighty and mysterious forces about
and above the life of man, appearing in the forms of
nature, while a natural basis of religion, is not in itself
religion; it may lead only to awe and fear and superstition, the creation of all the nature-worship of pagan-
ism, the elfin-brood of fairyland.

But when this sense of awe and mystery, this consciousness of the infinitude of life is held by a pure and humble soul, sensitive and meditative, above all one enlightened by the teachings of Christ, one expects to find the dim shadows of other and higher powers than self take the form or conception of an infinite life, that has thought and feeling and will.

There is everywhere in Wordsworth's poetry the tendency to seek to grasp the world as a whole, to rise above details to the center and soul of all phenomena, to infinite being, to the *one* infinite being. He carried the God-consciousness; and the interest in nature, the wealth of its unfolding, the joy and satisfaction in it was in that a spirit communed with his spirit. The poetry of Wordsworth is often thrilling with Divinity as Nature herself. "The Heart Leap Well" is the lesson of Jesus that the Father careth for the creatures of the earth.

> Gray-headed shepherd, thou hast spoken well;
> Small difference lies between thy creed and mine:
> This beast not unobserved by nature fell;
> His death was mourned by sympathy divine.
>
> The Being, that is in the clouds and air,
> That is in the green leaves among the groves,
> Maintains a deep and reverential care
> For the unoffending creatures whom he loves.

It is the spirit of Coleridge's "Ancient Mariner":

> He prayeth well who loveth well
>   Both man and bird and beast;
> He prayeth best who loveth best

> All things both great and small:
> For the dear God who loveth us
> He made and loveth all.

In the first part of the "Prelude," written early in his poetic work, immediately following the description of mysterious shapes and powers touching his life (already quoted), is this personal and spiritual interpretation:

> Wisdom and Spirit of the Universe!
> Thou *soul* that art the eternity of thought,
> That givest to forms and images a breath
> And everlasting motion, not in vain
> By day or star-light thus from my first dawn
> Of childhood didst thou intertwine for me
> The passions that build up our human soul;
> Not with the mean and vulgar works of man;
> But with high objects, with enduring things,—
> With life and nature, purifying thus
> The elements of feeling and of thought,
> And sanctifying, by such discipline,
> Both pain and fear, until we recognize
> A grandeur in the beatings of the heart.

Then in "Tintern Abbey," written about the same time, we have the noblest work of imagination in putting in immortal form the dim and vanishing sense of a spiritual presence that men so often have in the more beautiful or striking forms of the natural world.

> And I have felt
> A presence that disturbs me with the joy
> Of elevated thoughts: a sense sublime
> Of something far more deeply interfused,

Whose dwelling is the light of setting suns,
And the round ocean and the living air
And the blue sky, and in the mind of man:
A motion and a spirit, that impels
All thinking things, all objects of all thought,
And rolls through all things.   Therefore am I still
A lover of the meadows and the woods,
And mountains; and of all that we behold
From this green earth; of all the mighty world
Of eye and ear, both what they half create,
And what perceive; well pleased to recognize
In nature and the language of the sense,
The anchor of my purest thoughts, the nurse,
The guide, the guardian of my heart, and soul
Of all my moral being.

But is this conception of a Presence of such a nature, to use the words of Ex-President Patton, that if na-ture herself were destroyed, the Presence would remain? How can we know? How can we thus set the sharp, hard and fast lines of our Theism? If our thought is humble and reverent, how can we help the lines of our thinking shading off into the dim and indefinable. It may not be logic, but it is true to the soul's experience.

Now there are three ways of looking at our experience of the world of nature and life. It may be considered a mass of separate, unrelated facts, any connection between them a matter of accident or custom or association. This is the so-called atomic theory —"things are conjoined but not connected." It is of course atheistic. There can be no thought of God in a universe of chance. It is needless to say if such thought had possessed Wordsworth, he had not been the poet of nature. He was only

Contented, when with bliss ineffable
He felt the sentiment of Being spread
O'er all that moves and all that seemeth still.

Again, if things are not accidentally joined but connected by the idea of ends and order, then we must
think of a power beyond our experience, yet in it,
underlying all things and working through all things,
substantial and abiding. If this power is unconscious,
coming to consciousness only in man, then it is Pantheism.   The trouble, to use the language of John
Veitch, is to think of "a formless, indeterminate force
passing into the formed, definite, unending variety of
this beautiful world; of the conscious personality of
man rising out of the abyss of formless, undirected
energy."   Personality, and so freedom and responsibility are only haunting shadows. The ethic of Pantheism, higher or lower, is fatalism.

If this power underlying all things and working
in all things is conscious, conscious of itself and conscious of its workings, then it is a personal power
with thought and will, and this power is *God*.   It is
Theism, in whatever way you state or condition the
truth.   From this conscious power comes man,

From God who is our home,

and from this fact comes the significance to man of
the environing world.   On this simple distinction is
fixed Wordsworth's place as an immortal witness for
the Person and Presence of God.

The Presence of God! for the special grace of
Wordsworth's poetry is to make men conscious of God,
that God is in His world, and that its beautiful and

beneficent life demand Him and manifest Him.   He
was a Prophet of God to his generation.

And he came like all the other prophets, sent of God,
when there was great need of him.   For a long time
nature had been severed from God.   It was not so in
the teachings of prophets, of Christ and the Apostles.
The eastern Church still to a degree kept the thought
of God in life, but Augustine and still more his modern
disciple Calvin put stress upon the legal relations of God
and made His working a matter of law and not so much
of life.   Puritan theology had little sympathy with
nature.   Milton is an exception in his "Hymn to the
Nativity," in having the earth and the elements in harmony with the joy of the Incarnation.   Nature was
dark with the sin of man.   The very earth was cursed,
and the forest shades were peopled with evil spirits,
and the elements were the scourges of an angry God.
The first sermon of Davenport to the little colony of
New Haven was from the text, "Then was he led into
the wilderness to be tempted of the Devil."   It was a
natural reaction from this Puritan theology, an inevitable swing of the pendulum, to the deism and practical infidelity of the eighteenth century with its distant
God and its automatic universe.   You have but to take
up the formal and lifeless perfection of Pope to know
what nature and life are to the Poet without the She-
kinah.   "Life is only drest for show, mean handy-work
of craftsman, cook or groom."

> No grandeur now in nature or in book
> Delights us.

Wordsworth was a creative force in spiritual thought
as well as poetry.   He assailed Pope's mechanical view

of nature no less than his artificial view of verse. "He regarded it as his sacred mission to show that the world is full of beauty and meaning because it is throbbing with the life of God." He doesn't argue about God, any more than Jesus does; he suggests no didactic reasons for his Being; but he opens that inward eye which is the bliss of solitude, to the presence of the Infinite Life, to its beauty on the morning hills, its vitality in the "grandeur of the forest tree," the Presence

> Whose dwelling is the light of setting suns,
> And the round ocean and the living air,
> And the blue sky, and in the mind of man:
> A motion and a spirit, that impels
> All thinking things, all objects of all thought,
> And rolls through all.

The way to convince a man that there is music in Chopin (or any master) is to play, to truly interpret, one of his nocturnes, and his nature will respond to this breath of life. And so in the poetry of Wordsworth you feel the manifestation of God, His presence in the world that impresses itself upon the soul of the poet. You read with uncovered head; you go out as from the Presence Chamber. He is the poet of natural religion.

He can add nothing to the Theistic Conception of Christ. It may be said that without the personal revelation of God in Christ, we should not have the poet's sensitive nature and spiritual vision. But it is a great strengthener of faith, an enlargement of the spiritual life of men to be able to see with Wordsworth all created things tremulous with the life of God.

For the discerning intellect of man
When wedded to this goodly universe
In love and holy passion, shall find these
A simple product of the common day.

It is God's presence that is felt; not law but life.
It is the immanence of God, the truth that will make
nature the nurse of the soul. Wordsworth was the
prophet and teacher of this spiritual interpretation of
nature, the truth recently expressed of the supernatural in the natural: "I now conceive of God as
in His universe. I conceive of creation as a growth.
I conceive of Him as making the universe somewhat
as our spirit makes our body, shaping and changing
and developing it by processes from within. The
figures from the finite to the infinite are imperfect and
misleading, but this is the figure which best represents to me my own thought of God's relation to the
universe: not that of an engineer who said one morning, 'Go to, I will make a world,' and in six days or
six thousand years or millions of years, made one by
forming it from without, as the potter forms the clay
with skilful hand; but that of a Spirit who has been
forever manifesting himself in the works of creation
and beneficence in all the universe, one little work of
whose wisdom and beneficence we are and we see."
(Lyman Abbott.)
   Wordsworth's personal faith was very simple; it had
the simplicity of one who

              Mid all this mighty sum
              Of things forever speaking

had heard the voice of the great soul. "Theologians
may puzzle their heads about dogmas as they will; the

religion of gratitude can not mislead us. Of that **we** are sure; and gratitude is the handmaid to hope, and hope the harbinger of faith. I look abroad upon nature, I think of the best part of our species, I lean upon my friends, and I meditate upon the Scripture, especially the Gospel of St. John, and my creed rises up of itself, with the ease of an exhalation, yet a fabric of adamant."

Wordsworth wrote of the poets:

> Blessings be with them—and eternal praise,
> Who give us nobler loves, and nobler cares—
> The poets, who on earth have made us heirs
> Of truth and pure delight by heavenly lays!

And the prayer that his name might be **numbered** among theirs has certainly been answered.

His readers acknowledge the beneficent influence of his poetry. To love Wordsworth is the attainment of a pure and spiritual taste. The poetry of nature has a quieting effect upon the soul: it hushes the stormy passions into peace. The reading of his poems on nature is like going out from city streets, from its din and dust and glare, from the flitting of men and the grinding of rails,—to hills soft with forest green, along streams edged with cool thickets and meadows fringed with yellows and reds. It cools the fevered pulse and soothes the tired nerves, and tells us that life is not the mere tool or slave of toil and haste and gain, but a spirit still attended with gifts of beauty and joy.

> There is a blessing in the air,
> Which seems a sense of joy to yield
> To the bare trees, and mountains bare
> And grass in the green field.

To learn to love the poetry of Wordsworth is to gain a taste for *simplicity*. The love of show and power, the lust of the senses, that makes the complexity and strain of modern life, the gathering of its manifold trifles, is abashed before the eye that finds its wealth in the flower beneath the hedge, the colors of the sunset hills, the slowly upcurling mists,

> A host of golden daffodils.

> Wings have we, and as far as we can go
> We may find pleasure: wilderness and wood,
> Blank ocean and mere sky, support that mood
> Which with the lowly sanctifies the low.

It is a wonderful thing to feel the beauty of the world, to have a sense of its wondrous form and color and motion. Had Wordsworth done nothing more than help the vision of the beautiful, he had been among the richest gifts of song. And no man opens the eyes more than he does.

But above all he opens the eyes to the spiritual beauty of the world. He cultivates the devout spirit. He speaks of the first mild day of March,

> Each minute sweeter than before—

> Love, now an universal birth,
>   From heart to heart is stealing,
> From earth to man, from man to earth:
>   It is the hour of feeling.

> One moment now may give us more
>   Than fifty years of reason;
> Our minds shall drink at every pore
>   The spirit of the season.

Some silent laws our hearts will make,
    Which they shall long obey:
We for the year to come may take
    Our temper from to-day.

And from the blessed power that rolls
    About, below, above,
We'll frame the measure of our souls:
    They shall be tuned to love.

There's wisdom in the music of the woodland linnet.
The throstle is no mean preacher.

One impulse from a vernal wood
    May teach you more of man,
Of moral evil and of good,
    Than all the sages can.

Nature can so inform

The mind that is within us; so impress
With quietness and beauty, and so feed
With lofty thoughts, that neither evil tongues,
Rash judgments, nor the sneers of selfish men,
Nor greetings where no kindness is, nor all
The dreary intercourse of daily life,
Shall e'er prevail against us, or disturb
Our cheerful faith, that all which we behold
Is full of blessings.
While with an eye made quiet by the power
Of harmony, and the deep power of joy,
We see into the life of things.

CHAPTER III

A Poet of Democracy

CHAPTER III

Wordsworth was essentially a philosopher of human life. "His message from nature is wonderful, but his message from humanity is more profound." It can be said that he came to his human interest and knowledge through his love for nature. His youth was natural, joyous, one of a merry crew, fond of all the sports that took him into the open air, but he was not exceptional for his companionships; but he was exceptional for the mysterious spell over him of natural objects. Thus he came to regard objects outside of self and he soon came to regard men as an inseparable part of the environment of his own life. As he says in Michael:

> And hence this tale, when I was yet a boy
> Careless of books, yet having felt the power
> Of nature by the gentle agency
> Of natural objects, led me on to feel
> For passions that were not my own, and think
> On man, the heart of man, and human life.

As a youth, nature was a sensation, a satisfying delight; he "held unconscious intercourse with beauty," "drinking in a pure, organic pleasure," but with a man's reason, the interest in nature became deeper, for its impressions upon the mind, because of its message and ministry to the soul. It was the environment of man, and so the world had a new meaning to him.

> I have learned
> To look on nature, not as in the hour
> Of thoughtless youth; but hearing oftentimes
> The still, sad music of humanity.

Then we must remember that the years of his active manhood are from 1790 to 1830, years when the rights of man, the vision of a new society of man filled the thoughts of ardent, generous souls. "He grew up with the Revolution and survived it, and knew in life or rendered in art all its successive phases."

> Europe at that time was thrilled with joy,
> France standing on the top of golden hours,
> And human nature seeming born again.

The heart of Wordsworth was given to the people and his love was theirs.

> He looked with awe
> Upon the faculties of man; received
> Gladly the highest promises, and hailed
> As best, the government of equal rights
> And individual worth.

And though his dream was shattered of the speedy triumph of republican principles, and in seeming reaction he turned with pain and sadness from schemes of human rights to the isolation of the hills, he was true to his early vows, his heart was given to the people, and his love was never withdrawn. Though he was convinced that his mission was to be a poet and not to break his heart on the hard problems of civil rights, his poetry has been the noblest social force, working for the recognition of the essential worth of man. He has been called the "high priest of the new democracy." The lovers of Wordsworth have been lovers of men: they have been forces in the democratic movement.

As nature led Wordsworth to man, we notice that every character in his poems is associated with some natural object. The pictures of himself are connected with some scene of the outer world.

> The *poet* murmurs near the running brooks.
> He sits on that old gray stone.

Lucy

> dwelt among the untrodden ways
> Beside the Springs of Dove.

The gray rocks, the household lawn, the veil of trees, the fall of water, the little bay, the quiet road,—they are all together a part of the "Highland Girl,"

> Like something fashioned in a dream.

The leech-gatherer and the lonely moor are inseparable. Michael stands by the half-built sheepfold; and the pathos of Margaret is felt in the unkept garden and the red stains and tufts of wool on the cornerstone of the cottage porch, where the sheep were now permitted to come and couch unheeded. The unison of streams brings him comfort in the national sorrow at the hourly-expected death of Fox. When he first looked on Yarrow, he

> stood, looked, listened, and with thee,
> Great minstrel of the Border!

On the banks of the Nith, he

> asks of Nature, from what cause
> And by what rules
> She trained her Burns to win applause
> That shames the Schools.

In every case nature is the environment of the person or incident, as in life itself; the lines of character or action the sharper and more significant because of this realistic background. But nature is the inspirer of the thoughts of man. In this subtle sympathy and voicings of nature does the poet come to the conception of the significance of human life. But man is the chief thing. Man gives value to the encompassing world. This truth is vividly felt in the "Highland Girl."

There is a photograph taken by a seminary student of a mountain pass in Switzerland. Part way up this long sinuous line, lost at last among the peaks, stands a solitary figure. It was an artist's and a philosopher's instinct that took the view just at that moment. The distances can be measured by this human step. The man throws new light upon nature, and you feel that the meaning of all is wrapped up in the traveler trying to reach yonder height. It is a symbol of how Wordsworth came to human interest through his feelings for nature, and how the very significance of nature was found in its relation to the human spirit.

> Yea, what were mighty Nature's self?
> Her features, could they win us,
> Unhelped by the poetic voice
> That hourly speaks within us?

Not only are all the characters in Wordsworth's poetry connected with natural objects, but the most of them, and certainly the most significant are from *humble* life, such people as he met in the villages and along the ways of Westmoreland. A shepherd, a leech-gatherer, a reaper, a poor woman, a beggar, a little child. The hero of "The Excursion" is a peddler. Like Burns, he certainly built a princely throne on humble truth. And Wordsworth in his letters has given us a statement of the principle of this choice of subjects and of poetic language. "The principal object proposed in these poems, was to choose incidents and situations from common life, and to relate or describe them, throughout as far as possible, in a selection of language really used by men, and at the same time, to throw over them a certain coloring of imagination, whereby ordinary things should be presented to the mind in an unusual aspect; and further, and above all, to make these incidents and situations interesting by tracing in them, truly though not ostentatiously, the primary laws of our nature; chiefly, as far as regards the manner in which we associate ideas in a state of excitement. Humble and rustic life was generally chosen, because in that condition the essential passions of the heart find a better soil in which they can attain their maturity, are less under restraint, and speak a plainer and more emphatic language; because in that condition of life our elementary feelings coexist in a state of greater simplicity, and, consequently, may be more accurately contemplated, and more forcibly communicated; because the manners of rural life germinate from those elementary feelings, and, from the necessary character of rural occupations, are more easily comprehended, and are more durable;

and, lastly, because in that condition the passions of men are incorporated with the beautiful and permanent forms of nature." (App. vol. 2, p. 192.)

What was Wordsworth's interest in human life? His interest was not in the minute details of life about him. Everything of man did not concern him. He was a solitary figure among the hills, indulging in no neighborly gossip, not very approachable, not putting himself by sympathy into other lives, and so not greatly concerning himself about the interests and events of daily life. He did not write about humble men and women because of a humanity that responded to every event and every life.

Nor is he interested in the unfolding of character, the action of heredity upon environment, the soul at war with sense,—all that makes the passion and tragedy of human life. He has no dramatic instinct like Browning, the power to present a life in all the complexity of its nature and environment. Nor has he the lighter touch of Kipling, able to present realistically the outer action,—"a man in a world of men." "The Borderers," the only drama that Wordsworth attempted, was a dreary failure.

He has given us one of the finest love lyrics in "She was a phantom of delight," written of his wife; but it is the product of contemplation rather than passion, the verse of a man, who on his wedding trip could forget that he had a wife in his interest in studying inscriptions on tombstones. He is not lacking in intensity of feeling but it has been disciplined to flow in regular channels. The turbulent passions of life have settled into a fixed and orderly flow. His love is quietly domestic, like his skylark, true to the kindred points of heaven and home. It is impossible for

Wordsworth to have written the "Ae fond kiss and then we part" of Burns, or the "Last Ride Together" of Browning, or to have felt that tender and passionate clinging of true love in "John Anderson, my Jo, John" of Allan Cunningham; nor the passion of the "Bedouin Love Song" of Bayard Taylor:

> I love thee, I love but thee!
>   With a love that shall not die
>   Till the sun grows cold,
>   And the stars are old,
>   And the leaves of the Judgment Book unfold;

nor to have reached up to the immortality of love in Browning's "Prospice:"

>   I shall clasp thee again,
>   And with God be the rest.

Wordsworth's lines rarely beat with the elemental passions of man. His love flows in the channels of simple and quiet domestic joys. The modern poet of unrestrained feeling has little use for Wordsworth.

>   Morn into noon did pass, noon into eve,
>   And the old day was welcome as the young,
>   As welcome and as beautiful.

Wordsworth was too grave and serious a nature to laugh at the foibles and contradictions of human life. He lived in rather a small world of human incident. There is something of the provincialism of country life. Of the great world, of London, of fashion and traffic, of ambition and adventure, he knew little and cared less. As regards man he was more of an idealist than a realist. The man of the world, who is keenly comparing fractions with wholes, and is able to laugh or weep at the contrast, was not joined with the man of vision, as so often in modern literature, in Thackeray or Browning. *Punch* and *Life*, the children of laughter and mockery, had not been born. It is safe to say that if Wordsworth had had a little sense of humor, he would not have written many things, the lines, for example—

> And, whither art thou going, child,
> To-night, along these lonesome ways?
> To Durham, answered she, half wild,
> Then come with me into the chaise,

and called it poetry. However, we should never have had the view of man attended on his way with the vision splendid, if he had stopped to laugh. We must make our choice. We must accept the seriousness, if we would have the vision. And in this Wordsworth expressed the best life of his age. The sense of problem was too deep, the needs and hopes of men, for the leaders to forget the gravity of their purpose. "The great outburst of poetic idealism at the first of our own century is intensely grave. Peasant-fun and peasant-joyousness bubble through the lilts of Burns; but after his day, gravity settles down upon us. Of the poets of the Revolution only one is ever merry. Wordsworth's peddler in "The Excursion" assuredly never either made or took a joke; the blitheness of even his 'Highland Girl' is too reticent for outward mirth; while 'Peter Bell' and his ass tell us with every bray that they live in a world secure against invasions of laughter. There is no more irony nor absurdity in the poems of Shelley than in the sky at dawn. Coleridge, controlling the supernatural, grotesque, is yet devoid of genuine humor except in one or two political poems. So is Keats, though his seriousness is not moral but esthetic. One poet, and one alone, of that great early group, can to-day reach our affections through our amusement. If Byron lives, he lives by virtue of wit. The sorrowful recklessness of his irony bears the stamp of living power, unknown to his heroics or his sentimental tears."

And this brings us to the real message of Wordsworth as to man. He is the poet of the *essential worth of man*. He began as the advocate of the rights of man. He was an ardent demo*crat*. Titles and ranks, inherited distinctions and rights melted like snow before the ardor of his sympathies. The hope of man was in political action, and he dreamed of brotherhood. When that dream was ruthlessly shattered by the excesses of republicanism, and the poet was thrown back upon himself,—not to be a social and political leader but simply a poet,—trusting to the silent and pervasive influence of thought upon individual lives to make a new earth, he seemed to many lovers of liberty to take a reactionary course. As far as political faith, he was reactionary. He saw popular movements fathered by commercialism. There was a loss of reverence, and obedience. There was a vulgar pushing for rights without regard to worth. There was a rapid increase of wealth and vulgar display. The conceptions of life were materialized.

> We must run glittering like a brook
> In the open sunshine, or we are unblest—
> The wealthiest man among us is the best.

He lived at the beginning of the Industrial Revolution. The factory system drew men from quiet, rural life and crowded them into close, noisy, ugly, unwholesome towns. A restless competition put women and children to work in dark mines and in unsanitary buildings. It crushed the hope and beauty of life. And these changes were associated in Wordsworth's mind with the Whigs, the party of boasted progress. He heard men clamor loudly for reform, and talk bravely of the rights of the slave, who were unmindful of the fact that so-called progress was built on the sufferings of the poor. And so his thought as far as political action went, turned back to the older order. He became an advocate of authority; he was a Tory in politics. He opposed the Reform bill and other so-called democratic measures. He was a great advocate of the Established Church as a force for social order. And so there were those who felt that Wordsworth had betrayed the cause of human rights. Shelley felt so, who never knew Wordsworth, and who was always a poet of Revolution:

Poet of nature! thou hast wept to know
That things depart which never may return:
Childhood and youth, friendship and love's first glow,
Have fled like sweet dreams, leaving thee to mourn.
These common woes I feel. One loss is mine
Which thou too feel'st, yet I alone deplore,
Thou wert as a lone star, whose light did shine
On some frail bark in winter's midnight roar:
Thou hast like to a rock-built refuge stood
Above the blind and battling multitude:
In honored poverty thy voice did weave
Songs consecrate to truth and liberty,—
Deserting these, thou leavest me to grieve,
Thus having been, that thou should'st cease to be.

And Browning in his youth felt the same way and expressed the protest in verse, that only his manly regret in after years could blow away from Wordsworth's clear fame:

Just for a handful of silver he left us,
Just for a riband to stick in his coat—
Found the one gift of which fortune bereft us,
Lost all the others, she lets us devote;
They, with the gold to give, doled him out silver,
So much was theirs who so little allowed:
How all our copper had gone for his service!
Rags—were they purple, his heart had been proud!
We that had loved him so, followed him, honored him,
Lived in his mild and magnificent eye,
Learned his great language, caught his clear accents,
Made him our pattern to live and to die!
Shakspere was of us, Milton was for us,
Burns, Shelley were with us—they watched from their
      graves!
He alone breaks from the van and the freeman,
He alone sinks to the rear and the slaves!

We shall march prospering,—not through his presence:
Songs may inspirit us,—not from his lyre;
Deeds will be done,—while he boasts his quiescence,
Still bidding crouch whom the rest bade aspire:
Blot out his name, then, record one lost soul more,
One task more declined, one more footpath untrod,
One more devil's triumph and sorrow for angels,
One wrong more to man, one more insult to God!
Life's night begins; Let him never come back to us!
There would be doubt, hesitation and pain,
Forced praise on our part—the glimmer of twilight,
Never glad confident morning again!
Best fight on well, for we taught him—strike gallantly,
Menace our heart ere we master his own;

Then let him receive the new knowledge and wait us,
Pardoned in heaven, the first by the throne!

Such a poem, of which there is no finer scorn unless
it be Whittier's "Ichabod," shows the inevitable misconception, the disciplined, contemplative course of
Wordsworth met from the fiery temper of the revolutionary period. Browning was manly enough in after
years to confess his mistake, and to wish that his "Lost
Leader" might not henceforth be associated with
Wordsworth, but simply as an impassioned plea against
failure to follow the ideal. Lowell, who certainly was
a consistent republican, yes, almost a defiant republican,
says of Wordsworth: "I see no reason to think that
he ever swerved from his early faith in the beneficence
of freedom, but rather that he learned the necessity of
defining more exactly in what freedom consisted, and
the conditions, whether of time or place, under which
alone it can be beneficent, of insisting that it must be
an evolution and not a manufacture, and that it should
co-ordinate itself with the prior claims of society and
civilization. . . . He had made the inevitable discovery
that comes with years, of how much harder it is to do
than to see what 'twere good to do, and grew content
to build the poor man's cottage, since the means did not
exist of building the prince's palace he had dreamed."

Whatever his political action, his real sentiment
breathes in his verse and shows itself in his way of
living. He belonged to the plain people, as much as
Abraham Lincoln. He not only believed in poverty but
practiced it. "Plain living and high thinking" will
always be associated with him. He would not give
his heart away, with its true vision and pure feeling,
for any sordid boon of getting and spending. And by

virtue of his own simple and pure life, he was able to look through all the circumstance of place and garb and manner to the life itself. He saw noble life behind rough exteriors and hard faces. "His attitude is a tender, reverent, direct contemplation of essential man." He takes persons in the humblest circumstances, strips them of all adventitious helps, and shows some single trait of nobility. He cares less for clothes than the Teufelsdröckh of Carlyle. It has been said with much truth that his sympathies were rather *for* men than *with* them. It was not a question of natural likings but of fixed attitude of mind. The ethical nature was inseparably bound with the poet; and this kept him from fellowship with men whose ways he could not approve. But he had sympathy *for* men almost unlimited, felt contempt for no living thing, and was able to see the "heart of good in things evil." And wherever the poetry of Wordsworth has become a culture, it has worked for the deliverance of the nature from the bondage of convention, the false and artificial estimates of human pride and taste, and brought man into fellowship with his brother man.

If thou be one whose heart the holy forms
Of young imagination have kept pure,
Stranger! henceforth be warned; and know that pride,
Howe'er disguised in its own majesty,
Is littleness; that he who feels contempt
For any living thing, hath faculties
Which he has never used; that thought with him
Is in its infancy.

He says of the beggar:

'Tis nature's law,
That none, the meanest of created things,

Of forms created the most vile and brute,
The dullest or most noxious, should exist
Divorced from good—a spirit and pulse of good,
A life and soul, to every mode of being
Inseparably linked.

He not only teaches a reverence for human life, but a *reverence for law;* not law as the instrument of authority, the rule of tyrants, but law as the true course of a man's life, and the divine voice in human society. And so he shows us the glory of fidelity in humble spheres, and shows that stern duty

> dost wear
> The God-head's most benignant grace.

He teaches the soul, whatever be the hard lot, to admit of no decay.

> Brook no continuance of weak-mindedness.

He teaches fidelity to the whole self. His happy warrior is the man,

> Who, whether praise of him must walk the earth
> Forever, and to noble deeds give birth,
> Or he must go to dust without his fame,
> And leave a dead unprofitable name,
> Finds comfort in himself and in his cause.

But the praise of humble things and the path of lowly fidelity is not an opiate to lull men into low content. He feels the wrongs of men, he claims

> That virtuous liberty hath been the scope
> Of his pure song.

He invokes the spirit of Milton as the genius of English freedom:

> We are selfish men;
> Oh! raise us up, return to us again;
> And give us manners, virtue, freedom, power.
> Thy soul was like a star, and dwelt apart;
> Thou had'st a voice whose sound was like the sea:
> Pure as the naked heavens, majestic, free,
> So did'st thou travel on life's common way
> In cheerful godliness; and yet thy heart
> The lowliest duties on herself did lay.

Wordsworth is not universal in his sympathies like Shakspere and Browning in that he seems to touch every side of man's nature, all that is in man; but universal in that he touches some truth or capacity that is in all men. He regards each man as a part of humanity, for whom the wondrous ministry of nature and human life has been ordained; and teaches reverence and love, trust and fidelity, by which each life is to be measured and to make its contribution to the betterment of the whole. "He regards man," says the poet Aubrey de Vere, "not as a busy agent amid the turmoil of life, nor yet as an ascetic 'housed in a dream.' He regards him rather as a being in whom there unite countless mysterious influences both from the inner world of the spirit and from the visible creation of God, constituting, when thus combined, a creature destined for lofty contemplation, yet bound at the same time by a network of sympathies 'descending to the worm in charity.' If he looks upon human gladness, his ready sympathy with it is seldom unshadowed by a remembrance of the speed with which joy passes into sorrow; and when contemplating sorrow, his most abiding thought is that her mission is to cleanse, to elevate, and to make free. He sees good in all things; yet in all good things, he sees also some record of a higher good now lost, so that the rejoicing of man seems but the captive's harping in the land of exile. For him the smallest objects have rightful claims upon our deeper affections; yet the greatest are scarcely worthy of man's higher desires, for the potential excellences in them too often are but 'things incomplete and purpose betrayed.' "

Man, the humblest child, is worth regard because of his kinship to God. This is the source of Wordsworth's universal sympathy, that man has a divine nature. The imperfection of human life, its rough materials and broken forms, does not shake his faith. The world is still a-building, and God is working upon human lives. He raises the song of thanks and praise

> For those obstinate questionings
> Of sense and outward things,
> Fallings from us, vanishings;
> Blank misgivings of a creature
> Moving about in worlds not realized,
> High instincts before which our mortal nature
> Did tremble like a guilty thing surprised.

The truths of the soul, of its divine origin and relationship and destiny, are the

> truths that wake
> To perish never;
> Which neither listlessness, nor mad endeavor,
> Nor man nor boy,
> Nor all that is at enmity with joy,
> Can utterly abolish or destroy.

He interprets life in the light of his own high instincts
and so sees the divine in the commonplace and finds
noble lives in rough ways and untoward circumstances.

And lives that here only begin to grow shall else-
where have their perfection. The primal sympathy,
in which we had the beginning of our life, which binds
us to God, and from which spring soothing thoughts
in human suffering, this primal sympathy,

> Which having been must ever be

gives us

> The faith that looks through death.

The simple, rough lives are so interesting because they
are the creatures of the endless years. It is no unconscious immortality like George Eliot's "Choir Invisible," living in the growing life of mankind, in "lives
made nobler by our presence," but the continuance and
unfolding of a deathless personality. Nowhere has
Wordsworth expressed his simple faith in life beyond
death as in "The Primrose of the Rock."

> A Rock there is whose homely front
>   The passing traveler slights;
> Yet there the glow-worms hang their lamps,
>   Like stars, at various heights;
> And one coy Primrose to that Rock
>   The vernal breeze invites.
>
>   *   *   *   *   *
>
> Sin-blighted though we are, we too,
>   The reasoning Sons of Men,
> From one oblivious winter called

Shall rise, and breathe again;
And in eternal summer lose
Our threescore years and ten.

To humbleness of heart descends
This prescience from on high,
The faith that elevates the just,
Before and when they die;
And makes each soul a separate heaven,
A court for Deity.

Wordsworth is the poet of democracy because he sees and expresses the essential life and hope of every man. He is not downcast or forlorn because he sees ill sights of madding passions; he speaks of what we are, he dreams on things to come; and so he rouses the sensual from their sleep of death, and wins the vacant and the vain to noble raptures. His life expresses "the image of a better time, more wise desires and simple manners." William Watson has paid the fitting tribute to his master:

It may be that his manly chant, beside
More dainty numbers, seems a rustic tune;
It may be, thought has broadened since he died
Upon the century's noon;
It may be that we can no longer share
The faith which from his fathers he received;
It may be that our doom is to despair
Where he with joy believed;—

Enough that there is none since him who sings
A song so gotten of the immediate soul,
So instant from the vital fount of things
Which is our source and goal:

And though at touch of later hands there float
More artful tones than from his lyre he drew,
Ages may pass ere trills another note
  So sweet, so great, so true.

CHAPTER IV

Tennyson: The Man and the Poet

CHAPTER IV

TENNYSON: THE MAN AND THE POET

Six months after the death of Wordsworth, the laurel crown of English poetry was on the brow of Alfred Tennyson.

> This laurel greener from the brows
> Of him that uttered nothing base.

Is there between the two poets anything more than this slight outward connection of Laureateship? Is Tennyson a successor to the poetic spirit and work of the simple figure who

> Murmurs near the running brooks
> A sweeter music than their own?

Above all, is he a successor of the man who found in the humblest flower "some concord with humanity"?

Alike in their conception of the high calling of the poet, alike in their single-eyed devotion to the poet-life, "in the soul admitting of no decay, no continuance of weak-mindedness," had the right of naming his successor been given to Wordsworth, the mantle of the prophet would have fallen on no other than Tennyson. For of the latter he writes in 1845, before "The

Princess" or "In Memoriam" or the "Idylls of the King" had seen the light, "He is decidedly the first of our living poets, and I hope will live to give the world still better things."

It is not meant that Tennyson can be called in any proper sense a pupil of Wordsworth. He felt that in his best work Wordsworth was the successor of Shakspere and Milton, and often remarked that in the close, poetic interpretation of nature, Wordsworth was always before them. But "Tennyson is endowed precisely in points where Wordsworth wanted," says Emerson; "there is no finer ear, or more command of the keys of language." At times the voice seems that of Wordsworth, in its philosophic grasp of truth, in its true moral sense, and its perception of the subtle relation of nature and the human spirit. And again it is the haunting melody of Keats, and the glowing colors that thrill and satisfy the esthetic nature.

Tennyson had a catholic mind open to all comers. He was appreciative of what was best in contemporary work; he knew the noble succession of English song. Until he was seventeen Byron was his inspirer, but as he outgrew his passionate youth, he laid Byron aside and never cared for him again. He always felt that Keats had the richest endowment of any modern poet and would, had he lived, have fulfilled the promise of his youth. He was read in the world-poets, Homer, Æschylus, Theocritus, Virgil, Horace, Dante, Goethe, Schiller, and the French dramatists. Milton and Shakspere were his daily companions. "Where is my Shakspere? I must have my Shakspere," he said in his last illness. And he was buried with a copy of "Cymbeline" and a laurel wreath from Virgil's tomb. And yet none was his master. He was *composite,* the union of the poetic schools and influences that made the opening of the century an era rich in the sweetest and noblest poetry. His poetry is an "imaginative expression of life," not simply the personal expression of the poet (he was never so sensitive as towards the efforts of certain small critics to find his personal views and life in everything he wrote, notably in "Maud"), but to a very wide extent, almost a Shaksperean extent, the poetic form of the life of the age. The refined, speculative, questioning life; the minute, peering, aggressive life; the sensitive, believing, ministering life,—the complex life of the world-century is felt in his pages. And yet Alfred Tennyson is no imitator. While the age stands revealed, searched almost to its lowest consciousness in his pages, we feel all the time that a great interpreter is speaking. Everything is transformed in the alembic of his own spirit and genius. And he interprets because he touches life so widely and sympathetically and then meditates upon it so profoundly, and gives us so fearlessly and trustfully what God gives him to see.

The worth of Tennyson is not in his music, as sweet and varied as that is, the extraordinary perfection of form; but in the mass, variety and elevation of his thought. He is widely read, the most so of any English poet, because he is so clear and musical and varied; but he lives because he interprets life, to use the words of Matthew Arnold concerning Wordsworth, "because he deals with more of life than others; he deals with life as a whole more powerfully." And he interprets because he lives so largely and truly. The man is even greater than his work. "Artist and man moved together: his nature and his poetry are harmonious aspects of the same soul."

This is borne in upon anyone who reads the memoir by his son.   One lives in noble company.   One feels that

> The poet in a golden clime was born,
> *   *   *   *   *
> Dower'd with the hate of hate, the scorn of scorn,
> The love of love.

Above all one feels that

> He saw through life and death, through good and ill,
>   He saw through his own soul,
> The marvel of the everlasting will
>   An open scroll
>   Before him lay.

He interprets the thoughts of many hearts.   His poetry comes from his life as truly as the best sermon.   Poor as he was in his early years, he never would write a line for money.   Postponing for twelve years the thought of a home, and at times giving up the hope, he would not speak until he had a message and that message was put in its noblest form.   "The artist should do his best for art's sake, not for popularity," and this for *man's sake*.   He was one of the most unworldly men, yet with deepest interest in the world.   One of the most sensitive men, suffering from wrong conception, yet absolutely above the lust of praise.   He said of Alexander Smith: "He has plenty of promise, but he must learn a different creed to that he preaches in those lines beginning, 'Fame, Fame, thou art next to God.'   Next to God,—next to the Devil say I.   Fame might be worth having if it helped us to do good to a single mortal, but what is it?—only the pleasure of having oneself talked of up and down the street."

The reading of the life of Tennyson is a help to the higher life, and though he disliked the gossip and the personal matters often wrongly used in such books and never read them himself, holding that a true life is seen in its work, the life sheds light upon the work of the poet.

Wordsworth told a friend that he had not spent five shillings on new books in as many years; and of the few old ones that made up his collection, he had not read one fifth. He could never read Goethe and knew nothing of many of his contemporaries. His voice was pure and strong, but with something of the limitation of his singleness and isolation. Tennyson on the contrary is the "heir of all the ages." A diligent critic has found in the single poem of "In Memoriam" suggestions of twenty-six great minds, Greek, Latin, Italian, English,—historians, essayists, novelists, poets, and yet each made the gold of his own coin by being stamped with his experience,—as truly his own as the plays of Shakspere from the old chronicles of Holinshed. In Tennyson one understands how a great culture may minister to a great poet. Poetry was his profession, the serious business of his life from which nothing could divert him. He never suffered himself to waste his power in other things, in the doings of society or other kinds of work. And for poetry he prepared with large system and unwearied devotion, to master the materials and measures of his work. As poetry was the interpretation of life, and life in the nineteenth century meant not simply the life of Englishmen but the life of humanity, a world-life, he prepared himself to master the chief concerns of human interest: first the great poets of his own land and of European literature, the chief periods and persons of modern history, the sciences that were making a new earth and affecting the thoughts of men, politics as the vital questions of society, and above all the discussion of philosophy and theology, all the attempts to explain the meaning and duty of man.

So we find him, just from the University, not spending his days in dreaming, the occupation of the poet in the popular mind, but planning his week's study and holding to his plan, like a teacher or clergyman. And in the plan of those early studies were history, German, Italian, Greek, English poetry, chemistry, botany, electricity, mechanics, and theology. Soon after his marriage he took to reading different systems of philosophy. Spinoza, Berkeley, Kant, Schlegel, Fichte, Hegel, Ferrier were the books added to his already wide reading on such subjects. He knew that poetry must touch metaphysical subjects only by allusion, but he was not afraid of the highest problems that confronted men, and was anxious to know the fallacies that warped the minds of men and was resolute in proclaiming what seemed to him realities. Such studies are seen in his high thought, in such poems as "The Higher Pantheism," "In Memoriam," "De Profundis" and "The Ancient Sage." "He often brings up metaphysical truths from the deepest depths" is Jowett's word concerning him.

He was always a student of the Bible and eagerly read all notable books within his reach relating to the Bible, "and he traced with deep interest such fundamental truths as underlie the great religions of the world." He studied Hebrew that he might get the spirit of the Old Testament, particularly the Book of

Job, which he sometimes dwelt upon as a subject for modern poetry. He asked Jowett one day to read a line of Job which he did not quite understand, and when the great master of Balliol replied that he did not know Hebrew, Tennyson said with unfeigned surprise, "What! you a priest of a religion and not able to read your own sacred books!"

He not only had this large and generous culture that always went on, but he prepared long and thoroughly for any special work. The list of books that he read for his "Queen Mary" would dismay a historical lecturer. He was as careful as Macaulay to visit every scene connected with his characters. J. R. Green, the historian of the English people, said that "all his researches into the annals of the twelfth century had not given him so vivid a conception of the character of Henry II and his court as was embodied in Tennyson's Becket."

He worked his way into the sciences with the same patient thoroughness, so that men like Tyndall and Huxley, the Duke of Argyle and Lord Kelvin recognized the worth of his scientific opinions. "Since Dante no poet in any line so loved the stars," said a great astronomer. There were no mistakes about the stars or the flowers in his poems.

Thackeray declared that Tennyson was the wisest man he knew. It is a splendid testimony to the fact urged in the first chapter, that the wider the sphere of knowledge the wider the bounds of imagination, and it is the splendid tribute to the sphere of the poet that whatever concerns the human mind may be food for the imagination and through poetry may minister to the spiritual life of men.

Tennyson loved *nature* as truly as Wordsworth, but

in a different way. He loved nature for her own sake, the deep-voiced music of the pines, the crash and thunder of her seas upon the beach, the sweet notes of the thrush or the lark, the green vistas of wooded glades, the lights and shadows on the hills, the ominous muttering and flashing of the storm;—every form and power of the world he loved. It satisfied his sense of beauty; it quickened his questioning spirit; it subdued his mind with its awful mystery and power.

The first home of his own was in a London suburb, Twickenham, famous since the days of Pope; but he soon escaped from the distractions of city life to the quiet of the country, and he made a true poet's home at Farringford, the Isle of Wight, where he plowed his fields and planted his trees and cared for his flowers and shrubs with growing love for nearly half a century. In the last years of his life, through the residence of the Queen at Osborne, and so the world of fashion, and the attraction of his own great fame, bringing so many strangers to his doors, he felt compelled to make a new summer home at Aldworth, on the mainland, in a beautiful and retired section of west England where all things fair to view grew under his touch. Though he spent most of his life in the country, Tennyson was no recluse. He simply felt the imperious claim of his art to the whole of his energies, and "so was bound to abstain from the idle trivialities and current compliments of society." He found the largest and freest life for his art in the quiet of nature and books.

And not only was nature the opportunity for his work, but a satisfying companionship. It was all worthy of his thought and love. And he gave it the attention of his serious and trained mind. Not a flower or bird-note escaped his notice. As in Kingsley's case, it was the love of scientist and artist combined. He was not tracing as did Wordsworth the faintest marks of nature on the human mind; he was absorbed in the marks themselves on the face of nature. He loved the touch of nature's forces, the sun, the rain, the wind. He took his walks without regard to sun or storm, never protected save by his cloak and thick boots, rejoicing to feel the sun and the rain and to know that he was alive. And this love of life itself never grew old and dim. In the last spring of his life he "enjoyed as much as ever the blossoms of apple and pear tree, of white lilacs, and of purple aubretia that bordered the walks." He said that he did not believe in Emerson s pretty lines,

> Only to children children sing,
> Only to youth the Spring is Spring.

"For age does feel the joy of spring, though age can only crawl over the bridge while youth skips the brook."

Like Wordsworth he often composed in walking, and he took all his nature-similes direct from observation, though I do not think that like Wordsworth he depended upon nature for the quickening of his imagination. However, the outward suggestions are marked in Tennyson's poetry, and one is charmed with the exactness and variety and beauty of the images of nature.

One constantly hears the sea in his verse. The sea was his great passion, its changing beauty, its mighty force, its immeasurable mystery, its ceaseless music held him like an appetite. "He loved the sea as much as any sailor and knew all its moods whether on the shore or in midocean. He loved it for its own sake

and also because English heroism has ever been con-
spicuous on shipboard: he felt in himself the spirit of
the old Norsemen. His delight in the sea more especially comes out in such poems as "Enoch Arden,"
"Ulysses," "The Revenge," "The Voyage," "The
Sailor Boy," "Sea Dreams," "Maud," "Break, Break,"
and "Crossing the Bar"; and "I remember well," says
his son, "his glory in having made these lines in
'Boadicea':

"Fear not, isle of the blowing woodland, isle of silvery
    parapets;
Thine the liberty, thine the glory, thine the deeds to be
    celebrated,
Thine the myriad-rolling ocean, light and shadow illimi-
    table."

To my mind the most noticeable quality in the person of Tennyson was his *rich* and *generous humanity*.
Here he differed essentially from Wordsworth, in that
he loved men, and not simply the essential man. No
man ever had more or more devoted friends, the best
mark of his own nobility. At the University such
pleasant and inspiring fellowship, as Monckton Milnes,
poet and critic (afterwards Lord Houghton); Richard
Chenevix Trench (Archbishop of Dublin) poet and
Bible scholar; Dean Alford of Canterbury; W. H.
Brookfield, the dearest friend and ideal minister of
Thackeray; Charles Merivale, the historian of the Ro-
man Empire; James Spedding, a great Greek scholar;
Fitzgerald, the translator of Omar; and above all
Arthur Henry Hallam, the son of the historian, to
whom "In Memoriam" is the monument, monument
of both poet and friend, in the pure and lofty strains
of which the two are linked in love and fate. During

the ten years of silence from '32 to '42, when his genius was maturing its power, and his soul was working through the problems of sin and suffering to childlike trust, he was much in London and had the close friendship of such men as Cunningham, Carlyle, Gladstone, Mill, Thackeray, Forster, Sterling, Landor, Macready. And later came the rich friendship of Browning and Palgrave, Jowett and Argyle. The most distinguished literary and scientific men in England were his friends. And he opened his heart especially to men in the Church or without who had new light to throw upon the problems of life and destiny. His homes at Farringford and Aldworth were open to his friends, and here hundreds were welcomed with simple and genuine hospitality.

His warm and generous friendships were expression of a heart that beat true for all men. He was hailed at first by a select few and this by the richness and strangeness of his melody. But it was not the mind of Tennyson to be the pet of the drawing-room. He soon worked free from such misconception. He let the world know that he felt for "men the workers, men my brothers." He agreed with Mazzini that "nothing in this world is so contemptible as a literary coterie." He always delighted in the "central roar" of London, and the first thing he did on entering the city was to walk the Strand and feel the touch of common life. As young men, he and Arthur Hallam often discussed the problems of the poor. "The unsettled condition of the country, and the misery of the poorer class weighed upon them. It seemed difficult to young men, starting in life, to know how to remedy these evils, but they determined not to lose hold of the real in seeking the ideal." Hallam writes, "When the ideas of time and sorrow are not, and sway not the soul with power, then is no true knowledge in Poetry or Philosophy."

He sympathized with every rational effort for larger life for men. He rang the Church bells at midnight on the passage of the Reform Bill of 1832, much to the horror of the Tory rector who had followed his father. He could not bear any haughty spirit towards the poor or superciliousness towards their efforts for liberty. Dean Bradley of Westminster Abbey describes a garden party, where, after eating plentifully of peaches, some one to a remark about the possible disagreement of the fruit replies jocularly about "the disturbed districts," alluding of course to some disorders apprehended or existing in the centers of industry. "I remember being startled by your father's voice and accent, 'I can't joke about so grave a question,' and thinking to myself that it was exactly what one so different as Dr. Arnold might have said under similar circumstances." He always had special care about courtesy to the poor, and the severest punishment he ever gave his son was for want of respect to one of the servants.

The humanity of Tennyson gives his poems their universal note. He sings of the common loves and hopes and struggles of men. He pictures the heroic element of common life. He lifts the heart to the great thoughts of home and country and God.

> He sings of what the world will be
> When the years have died away.

And so he helps men everywhere. A Gordon shut up in Khartum can say, "The reading of Tennyson has been my great relief," and a poor workman unable to

buy the volumes learns some of the poems by heart
and repeats them for support in toil. He is the poet
of the people.

Plowmen, shepherds have I found, and more than once, and
    still could find,
Sons of God and Kings of men in utter nobleness of mind.

And Tennyson never lost this sympathy with the people. He constantly turned the conversation to the
problems of society. He was especially interested in
efforts at industrial coöperation. He did not the least
mind if England, when the people are less ignorant and
more experienced in self-government, eventually becomes a democracy. But he feared violent, selfish,
unreasoning democracy. And sometimes when he saw
society, vicious, and the poor starving in great cities,
he felt as though a mighty wave of evil were passing
over the world. It might be expected that the poet
of the second Locksley Hall would have a soberer vision
and more conservative spirit than the fiery youth of
twenty-two whose watchword was

Forward, forward, let us range,
Let the great world spin forever down the ringing grooves
    of change.

The word of progress he is still willing to use, but with
a higher meaning. He looks forward, but upward also.

Lame and old and past his time and passing now into the
    night;
Yet I would the rising race were half as eager for the
    light.

Mr. Tennyson was a deeply *religious* man, not religious in the sense of devotion to creed or Church,—of these he was not unmindful,—but religious in the more spiritual sense that his whole life was dominated by the thought of God. Men are really tested by their unconscious moments, that is, in the moments when the mind released from the tension of work, like an unbent bow springs back to its normal state. What are the feelings of men, what do they think about in these informal, unguarded moments? Here is revealed the real disposition of man. And by this sure test Mr. Tennyson stands out as a God-possessed man. With his friends, sooner or later he talked about the deeper problems of the soul. In his letters and journals the most significant things are questions of religion. Writing of the mechanic influence of the age and its tendency to crush and overpower the spiritual in man, he says, "What matters it how much man knows and does if he keeps not a reverential looking upward? He is only the subtlest beast in the field." "I hate utter unfaith," he would say. "I cannot endure that men should sacrifice everything at the cold altar of what with their imperfect knowledge they choose to call truth and reason. One can easily lose all belief, through giving up the continual thought and care for spiritual things."

"He had a sympathy with those who were impatient of the formal statement of truth, only because he felt that all formal statements of truth must of necessity fall below the greatness and the grandeur of the truth itself." So he was comprehensive in sympathies, trying to find the basis of all religion, in the spiritual nature of man, convinced that if men would stand together on this primal and simple basis, they would be soon found together in their practical allegiance to Christianity. So the main testimony to Christianity was not in miracles, but in that eternal witness, the revelation of what might be called the mind of God in the Christian morality and its correlation with the divine in man. At the same time he would say that Christianity with its divine morality but without the central figure of Christ, *the* Son of Man, would become cold, and that the spiritual character of Christ is more wonderful than the greatest miracle. The Duke of Argyle declares Tennyson the man of the noblest humility he had ever known. "It was not that he was unconscious of his own powers or indifferent to the appreciation of others." But it was that he was far more continually conscious of the limitations upon them in face of those problems of the universe with which in thought he was continually dealing. In his inner spirit he seemed to me to be always feeling his own later words:

> But what am I?
> An infant crying in the night:
> An infant crying for the light:
> And with no language but a cry.

Tennyson's father was gifted and versatile, a clergyman, poet, artist, musician, scientist, and from him no doubt he inherited much of his genius. His mother was no less remarkable for the depth and purity of her piety, and it is the influence of mother and home, and his own home and wife no less, that make his poems the constant idealization of womanhood and the beauty and purity of wedded love. And he confessed that he referred to his own mother in the words of "The Princess":

Happy he
With such a mother! faith in womankind
Beats with his blood, and trust in all things high
Comes easy to him, and though he trip and fall
He shall not blind his soul with clay.

There is a beautiful letter from this mother, written in her old age, that is really a prayer for her son: "How fervently have I prayed for years that our merciful Redeemer would intercede with our Heavenly Father, to grant thee His Holy Spirit to urge thee to employ the talents He has given thee by taking every opportunity of endeavoring to impress the precepts of His Holy Word on the minds of others. My beloved son, words are too feeble to express the joy of my heart in perceiving that thou art earnestly endeavoring to do so."

One can see that the mother's prayer was abundantly answered as the attempt is made to trace the development of Tennyson's work through the years. The first poems of 1827 (the two brothers) when he was eighteen, are full of melody, but with only faint prophecies of his spiritual insight. The first volume of his own poems, 1830, the second year at Cambridge, containing such poems as "Lilian," "Marian," "The Poet," illustrate the first characteristics of his genius, an exquisite sense of the charms of sound and rhythm based on an earnest capacity for sober thought. The second volume, 1832, containing "The Lady of Shalott," "The Lotus Eaters," "The Palace of Art," and "A Dream of Fair Women," shows the same fine regard for melody but a greater desire to build on worthy thought. "The Palace of Art" is the sin of a self-centered soul and strikes the note that grows richer and fuller that life should move in the love of truth, the truth of love.

The ten years of silence, under the shadow of a great affliction, were God's discipline for a spiritual prophet. The volume of 1842, containing such poems as "Locksley Hall," "Ulysses," "The Two Voices," "Sir Galahad," "The Vision of Sin," shows how his comprehension of human life had grown. Chivalry, duty, reverence, human passion, simple faith, the many complex moods of the religious nature were dealt with without "any brooding self-absorption." "It was the Humanities and the truths underlying them that he sang, and he so sang them that any deep-hearted reader was made to feel through his far-reaching thought that those Humanities are spiritual things, and that to touch them is to touch the garment of the Divine." Then followed one after another the noble works on which his fame chiefly rests: "The Princess," with lines that haunt the memory and songs as sweet as our tongue contains, and in the discussion of woman the example of his intellectual and spiritual sensitiveness to life-themes and his clear and brave vision of truth; "In Memoriam," the analytical study of the psychology of sorrow and the most religious poem since "Paradise Lost"; "Maud," the antiphonal voice to "In Memoriam"; "The Idylls of the King," the epic of Christian chivalry; "Mary," "Harold," and "Becket," the trilogy of English historical drama. In his last volume, "The Death of Œnone," we expect to read:

Spirit, nearing yon dark portal at the limit of thy human
     state,
Fear not thou the hidden purpose of that Power Who alone
     is great,
Nor the myriad world, His shadow, nor the silent opener
     of the gate.

His genius and his faith were both full to the end, and as he passed from earth in the flood of moonlight that filled the room and covered the great landscape outside, the watchers felt that his last word had been realized:

> Sunset and evening star,
> And one clear call for me!
> And may there be no moaning of the bar,
> When I put out to sea;
>
> But such a tide as moving seems asleep,
> Too full for sound and foam,
> When that which drew from out the boundless deep
> Turns again home.
>
> Twilight and evening bell,
> And after that the dark!
> And may there be no sadness of farewell,
> When I embark;
>
> For though from out our bourne of Time and Place
> The flood may bear me far,
> I hope to see my Pilot face to face
> When I have crossed the bar.

The poet of his youth was

> Bravely furnished all abroad to fling
> The winged shafts of truth.

And one couplet of the second "Locksley Hall," written fifty-six years later, and put on the tablet to the memory of the poet's son, Lionel Tennyson, is the poetic embodiment of the Laureate's life:

Truth—for truth is truth—he worshipped, being true as he
    was brave.
Good—for good is good—he followed, yet he looked be-
    yond the grave.

CHAPTER V

In Memoriam: The Way of Faith

CHAPTER V

IN MEMORIAM: THE WAY OF FAITH

The last chapter showed the nature and training of Tennyson as the preparation of a great poet, and especially for his interpretation of the spiritual life of man.

This interpretation is constantly made. Whatever the subject, he is inclined to reveal the very spirit of life. But it is most notable in two groups of poems, (1) the series of epics that are called "The Idylls of the King," and (2) in the lyrics that are gathered into "In Memoriam."

In the "Idylls" he takes the elementary virtues of men, integrity, endurance, honor, loyalty, represented in the persons and acts of early chivalry, touches them with a Christian light, and lifts them like a banner against a self-loving, deceptive, materialistic age. He felt that a lofty example that would touch the true pride of race and make conscience king was the great need of the world.

In "In Memoriam" he brought the faith of men to the test of the growing scientific and philosophical knowledge of nature and life, and connected the claims of Christianity with the problems of our daily experience.

Such is the spiritual meaning of "In Memoriam." It is the path experience takes to reach faith in immortality.

Break, break, break,
On thy cold gray stones, O Sea!
And I would that my tongue could utter
The thoughts that arise in me.

*   *   *   *   *

Break, break, break,
At the foot of thy crags, O Sea!
But the tender grace of a day that is dead
Will never come back to me.

Such was Tennyson in 1833, pouring forth in plain-
tive tones the sorrows of his widowed heart. His nature seemed to be overborne by grief. The only use
of his art, the only expression of his life to utter the
sad thoughts that arose in his heart.

Seventeen years pass and a different song is heard
from his lips, a hymn of calm and triumphant faith:

Strong Son of God, immortal Love,
Whom we that have not seen Thy face,
By faith, and faith alone, embrace,
Believing where we cannot prove;

*   *   *   *   *

Thou seemest human and divine,
The highest, holiest manhood Thou.
Our wills are ours, we know not how;
Our wills are ours, to make them Thine.

These songs, the first of personal grief, its unlight-
ened thought bent down upon the earth and its mournful cadences, the second turned upward to the Lord
of Love and outward to the larger hope for mankind,

stand as the landmarks of spiritual progress, the beginning and the end of that deep soul-experience whose perfected poetic expression is "In Memoriam."

Poetic tributes to friendship are apt to be narrow in theme and brief in influence. A life that has been kindred to one soul may be stranger to the multitude, and the note of sorrow or religious sentiment easily falls into wearisome routine.

The fact that "In Memoriam," the longest monody of English poetry, the most distinctly religious poem since "Paradise Lost," has constantly grown since the day of publication, 1850, to the present in thoughtful appreciation and profound influence until it seems at last to be, in the words of the poet himself, "the voice of the human race speaking through him," shows the greatness of Tennyson's genius and the interpretive power of his spirit.

" 'In Memoriam' is perhaps the richest oblation ever offered by the affection of friendship at the tomb of the departed," is the early judgment of Gladstone. And thirty years later, 1889, we read such words as these from the well-known Dante student Thomas Davidson: "Though I have been familiar with the poem from boyhood, it is only in the last few years that the full import of that problem and of the noble solution offered by the poet has become clear to me. The work, as I now understand it, seems to me not only the greatest English poem of the century,—which I have always believed,—but one of the great world-poems, worthy to be placed on the same list with the 'Oresteia,' the 'Divina commedia' and 'Faust.' " (Prolog.)

"In Memoriam" demands our study for its relation to the growth of the poet's genius; for its relation to the philosophic and religious movements of the age;

and for its attempted solution of the deepest and most vital problems of the human heart.

I

THE RELATION OF "IN MEMORIAM" TO THE POET'S GROWTH

The immediate effect of the publication of "In Memoriam" in 1850 was to direct study to the earlier poems of Mr. Tennyson for promise and growth of the power now manifested.

We have seen that in the earliest poems there was a basis of earnest thought, often covered by the artistic richness of coloring and melody, "the dainty finish, the minute painting of mosses and flowers, and the super-subtle shading of emotions." In 1842 the ten years of silence were broken by more manly notes. There is the same lyric freedom, the same delicacy of imagination, the same artistic choice of words. But strength is no longer concealed: it grasps and vitalizes all. Touch after touch has brought out the picture of "The Palace of Art," the sin of the self-centered soul. In "The Two Voices" and "The Vision of Sin," he deals with the crisis-experience of the soul; the significance of temptation and suffering, the reality of goodness, the mysteries of life and death; and he meets them with earnest and manly contentions for victory. He is no less the artist, but is more the man, the man with the prophet's vision and sympathy. He has learned the lowly lessons of the "cot in the vale," the lessons of human need and struggle. He can write such virile poems as "Ulysses":

'Tis not too late to seek a newer world.

He is profoundly stirred by the problems of the race. He is no longer, even unwittingly, the voice of a petted and select few, but the voice of the generation. He has learned to feel with

Men, my brothers, men, the workers;

to care for all that touches their welfare; to rejoice in the triumphs of true liberty; to thunder in scorn and wrath against the social tyrannies that crush the souls of men, and

The social lies that warp us from the living truth.

In such poems as "The Princess" he had revealed the "good at the heart of endless agitation," and struck the chord of social consciousness and hope.

Then comes the statlier Eden back to men:
Then reign the world's great bridals, chaste and calm:
Then springs the crowning race of humankind.

How are we to account for this growth, intensive and extensive, in depth of thought and sweep of sympathy? It is not solely the result of conscientious study and honest self-criticism, though no poet has ever made himself more the master of the history and art of his calling. It is not simply the natural growth of the "great and deep strength" with which he was dowered, the unfolding of the principles of thought and conduct in which he was bred, rich and noble as both these were. Forces beyond his choice and control also had to do with his training. "God calls his noblemen from the highlands of trial."

The words at the head of the poem, "In Memoriam, A. H. H. Obiit MDCCCXXXIII" reveal the secret of the profoundest changes in the thought and work of the poet.

Alfred Tennyson and Arthur Henry Hallam, fellow-students at Trinity College, Cambridge, were kindred spirits, aspiring, poetic natures, and grew together with the love

> More than my brothers are to me.

It was the wish of Tennyson to publish his volume of poems (1830) jointly with his friend Hallam after the example of the "Lyrical Ballads" of Wordsworth and Coleridge. They were rivals for the same college honors without envy, and went everywhere "joined and inseparable." It was Hallam who believed in the genius of his friend, and published the first favorable criticism of his poems. All unite in the praise of the pure and promising career of young Hallam.

> High nature amorous of the good,
> But touch'd with no ascetic gloom.

His sudden death in Vienna in 1833, while on a tour of the Continent with his father, the distinguished historian, was a terrible shock to Tennyson and left an abiding impression upon his nature.

> Behold the man that loved and lost,
> But all he was is overworn.

Seventeen years passed before love and sorrow received its last and highest expression in "In Memoriam"; years of questioning and conflict, of upreaching and growth; years of "dull hopeless misery and rebellion, passing up to the dawn of hope, acquiescent trust and calm happiness." Suffering had forced the soul to "front the realities of our mysterious life" and many a question had been raised and answered.

As early as 1842 others saw the changed art and traced the cause. "Much has he thought, much suffered," writes Margaret Fuller, "since the first ecstasy of so fine an organization clothed all the world in rosy light. He has not suffered himself to become a mere intellectual voluptuary, nor the songster of passion and fancy, but has earnestly revolved the problems of life and his conclusions are calmly noble." And Carlyle calls him "a right valiant, true-fighting, victorious heart," and calls upon all other men to be thankful and joyful for the "note of eternal melodies in this man." And we have the poet's own testimony to the deepened change in the fifth and sixth stanzas of the Epilogue:

> Regret is dead, but love is more
>   Than in the summers that are flown,
>   For I myself with these have grown
> To something greater than before;
> Which makes appear the songs I made
>   As echoes out of weaker times,
>   As half but idle brawling rhymes,
> The sport of random sun and shade.

It may be said that suffering had its true influence upon a noble life, in opening the poet's soul to the manifold voices of truth, in making his nature sensitive to the conflicting forces and problems of the generation.

> My pulses therefore beat again
>   For other friends that once I met:
>   Nor can it suit me to forget
> The mighty hopes that make us men.

II

In the opening chapter, the creative forces of the century were given, that would inspire poetry. Now it is well briefly to suggest the particular relation of "In Memoriam" to these forces, to the *philosophic* and *religious movements* of the generation.

There is no more vital or germinant epoch in the history of English thought than from 1825 to 1845. The application of invention to steam and electricity was revolutionizing industry. The deeper study of science, in both nature and man, was leading to new theories of life and of human progress. The philosophic mind of Germany was quickening that of England. It was the age of the Reform Bill, the age of political and social and religious agitations. In the language of John Morley: "A great wave of humanity, of benevolence, of desire for improvement, a great wave of social sentiment, in short, poured itself among all who had the faculty of large and disinterested thinking."

Coleridge was the first and most directive mind of the epoch. In his "Aids to Reflection" he makes his appeal to the spiritual consciousness of men and insists upon the certitude of faith. Arnold and Whately, his disciples, were instruments for enlarging the traditional views of the Scriptures and the Church and for bringing men to feel that the spiritual life consisted of daily contact with the Divine Spirit rather than adherence to particular form or party. And Christianity has shown a nobler spirit ever since.

It is the spirit of the larger intellectual and spiritual freedom that speaks in Tennyson.

> Our little systems have their day:
> They have their day and cease to be:
> They are but broken lights of Thee,
> And Thou, O Lord, art more than they.

It is the Coleridgian distinction between knowledge and faith that meets us in "In Memoriam": the reassertion of the spiritual nature of man that says of knowledge:

> What is she, cut from love and faith,
> But some wild Pallas from the brain
> Of Demos? . . .
> She is the second, not the first.
> For she is earthly, of the mind,
> But wisdom heavenly, of the soul.

Carlyle was a member with Tennyson of the Sterling Club and a lifelong friend, and they constantly discussed the most vital questions. As to historical Christianity I suppose it must be confessed that Carlyle's influence is largely negative; but he hated shams, and made direct appeal to conscience and had faith in the worth of man's intuitions. "In all human hearts there is the religious fiber," he would say, and so in a wide sense he was a spiritual teacher and made a wider place for religion in literature and in life. He was a prophet especially to a group of young men who "were determined to have done with insincerity, to find ground under their feet, to let the uncertain remain uncertain, but to learn how much and what we could honestly regard as true." And nowhere is this feeling of honest and fearless search more truly expressed than by Tennyson.

> You tell me doubt is devil-born.

> I know not: one indeed I knew
>   In many a subtle question versed,
>   Who touch'd a jarring lyre at first,
> But ever strove to make it true;

> Perplex'd in faith, but pure in deeds,
>   At last he beat his music out.
>   There lives more faith in honest doubt,
> Believe me, than in half the creeds.

Opposed to these idealists, these teachers of spiritual consciousness, stands another friend of Tennyson, John Stuart Mill, the sensationist and necessitarian. Holding that necessity sways man and nature, that the senses are the sole source of knowledge, he denied intuition, refused to believe the mind anything more than refined matter, and did not, except in moments of inconsistent feeling, find the idea of God possible in the universe. It is useless to deny Mill's influence in modern thought. It is the philosophy of George Eliot's fiction and Herbert Spencer's essays. To be sure, it has lost something of the baldness of its denial, but is none the less anti-spiritual under the milder garb of the agnostic.

> Tennyson would not make his judgment blind;
>   He faced the spectres of the mind.

He could state the baldest postulates of materialism and in the shadow of his sorrow he felt the chill of their merciless logic. He makes Nature say:

> Thou makest thine appeal to me:
>   I bring to life, I bring to death:
>   The spirit does but mean the breath:
> I know no more.

But his heart revolts against the denials of the spiritual nature.

> And he, shall he
> Man, her last work, who seem'd so fair,
>   Such splendid purpose in his eyes,
>   Who roll'd the psalm to wintry skies,
> Who built him fanes of fruitless prayer,
>
> Who trusted God was love indeed
>   And love creation's final law—
>   Though nature, red in tooth and claw
> With ravin, shrieked against his creed—
>
> Who loved, who suffer'd countless ills,
>   Who battled for the True, the Just,
>   Be blown about the desert dust,
> Or seal'd within the iron hills?
>
> No more? A monster then, a dream,
>   A discord. Dragons of the prime,
>   That tare each other in their slime,
> Were mellow music match'd with him.
> O Life as futile, then, as frail!

In the conflict of systems the softening of traditional views, the fourth decade of the century marks a transition. The religious formalism on the one hand, the skeptical languor on the other, were broken by two groups of men: the Oxford movement against the so-called progress of thought by exalting the authority of the Church, High-Church; the other (which might almost be called the Cambridge movement) or the Broad Church group, accepting new light from every source, made religion real and vital by renewing its forms and its service with the spirit of Christ.

Frederick Denison Maurice and Charles Kingsley were the soul of this stronger and broader religious life. Maurice was the theologian, the teacher, the prophet: Kingsley the poet, the novelist, the preacher: both eager in their search for truth, open-minded, loyal to their conviction. They cared not for the honor of men and carried their loftiest visions into the commonest duties. Their peculiar influence it seems to me was in the enlarging the sphere of spiritual life.

Tennyson, the devoted friend of Maurice and Kingsley, having like all who knew him well a peculiar reverence for Maurice and calling him his religious Master, was powerfully affected by this religious tendency; more than this, he gave to it the power of the noblest poetic form.

"Strong Son of God, Immortal Love" may be taken as the very keynote of the movement; and the closing verse of "In Memoriam" is the best summary of its thought:

> That God, which ever lives and loves,
>   One God, one law, one element,
>   And one far-off divine event,
> To which the whole creation moves.

Thus we see that "In Memoriam" is the articulation of the age-spirit in religion. So true is it, that we find the very words of the poem are constantly used: they have become the language of the noblest thought and hope of the age.

III

Now we turn to the most important questions of the poem, its purpose, its outline of thought, and its treatment of those religious truths which "every thinking man is trying to connect with his every-day experience." "In Memoriam" in the first and simplest view is a lament for a friend and as such it has often suggested comparison with the two other great elegies of English poetry, the "Lycidas" of Milton and the "Adonais" of Shelley. They are similar in subject, the sorrow for the loss of a dear friend cast off in youth: they are alike in the causes of sorrow, the loss of companionship, the withheld completion of life. But with this formal and outward comparison, the likeness ends. "Lycidas" and "Adonais" speak in classic form; "In Memoriam" in the person of the poet, direct and simple. The poems of Milton and Shelley are consistent and complete elegies, throughout the mourning for the dead: the poem of Tennyson is elegiac only in the beginning: it makes sorrow but the starting-point for the discussion of the mysteries of life and death.

The comparison is sometimes made between "In Memoriam" and the sonnets of Shakspere, suggested by the thought evidently in Tennyson's mind in the lines

I loved thee spirit, and love, nor can
The soul of Shakspere love thee more.

The parallelism is superficial. The sonnets of Shak-spere picture a love that is earthly, and touched with earth's sin and shame. But in "In Memoriam" love is idealized, fixed beyond estrangement and hallowed by death.

Mr. Thomas Davidson has made a still more striking comparison with the work of Dante : " 'In Memoriam' is the record of the shattering and rebuilding of a moral world in a man's soul. It belongs to the same class of works as the 'Divine Comedy' and 'Faust': only whereas the first of these is epic and the second dra-matic, this is lyric. The hero of 'In Memoriam,' like the hero of the 'Divine Comedy,' is the poet himself. Both poems are idealized records of actual experiences. In both the person beloved dies young, leaving the lover for a time utterly desolate. In both cases this desola-tion, instead of overwhelming the lover, finally quickens his spiritual perceptions, so that he is able to find in the spiritual world what he has lost in the material. In both cases, a pure, reverent human love leads the soul of the lover up to God. Dante finds again his lost Beatrice in the imaginary paradise of his time : Tenny-son finds his Arthur 'mix'd with God and nature.' In both poems the fundamental thought is the same : man's true happiness consists in the perfect conformity of his will with the Divine will, and this conformity is attained through love, first of man and then of God."

Many analyses of "In Memoriam" have been pub-lished in this country and in England. Professor Davidson's is perhaps the most philosophical and inter-pretive; Professor Genung's the most elaborate and minute. No one can work his way through the second without arriving at a finer appreciation of the poem. The trouble with it, however, is that no such unity of elaborate design was in the mind of the poet. We find from the life of Tennyson that the 131 separate poems that have been gathered into "In Memoriam" were written at different times through the seventeen years, each with no thought of publication as a collected whole, simply the natural and necessary expression of his heart, lest the "o'erfraught heart should break," each written at the suggestion of some natural object or recurring anniversary, or memory of his friend, or the phase of feeling, the expression of growing experience of the problem of death and suffering, its effect upon the individual and so its work for society.

These were written without thought of a whole, and so without definite plan. No doubt the Divine Spirit whom his devout mother invoked for his aid, no doubt the Immortal Love whom the Poet himself invokes to forgive his sin and grief,

> —his wild and wandering cries,
> Confessions of a wasted youth,

to

> Forgive them where they fail in truth,
> And in Thy wisdom make them wise

were answered in directing the soul and voice of the poet to a goal he could not wholly foresee. He was led by faith. There is a unity in the poem: it is found in the immortality of love, that holds the soul true through the storm and stress of sorrow and doubt, and brings it forth into a peaceful land, where a heavenly glory dwells and men take heart for a nobler future for themselves and for mankind. And so the poem is a devout guide to rational faith.

The only plan that Tennyson himself would admit is the simple division formed by the three Christmas seasons, at poems 28, 78, 104. This gives "In Memoriam" an introduction, 1-28, and three divisions or cycles. And it is not hard to find certain things in each cycle that seem to be characteristic, to trace certain steps of experience that seem to mark the onward movement of the whole.

The impression of the first cycle, 28-78, is found in "the aimless moods of sorrow," and the momentary gleams of hope darkened by doubt. Its prevailing tone is that of grief. The very poems are a "sad mechanic exercise" by which he would try to numb his pain.

> In words, like weeds, I'll wrap me o'er
> Like coarsest clothes against the cold.

Arthur loved to speak of divine things, but human grief dims the eye. The fact that we do not forget, lose our personality in sleep, does it not suggest that death may be only a sleep? But men want not a sleep, an absorption into the all, but a conscious life hereafter. What value in the mere fact of the life hereafter unless we are sure of its blessedness? Here is the terrible fact of evil. Who would care for an immortality of sin? Is there not hope that evil itself is a discipline and far off may be turned into good? Before these mysterious problems, we are but children crying in the night. Though we have no language but a cry, the desire for the future good of all is the most divine thing in us. Is it a ray of the divine light? Nature cannot tell us, she is callous to these motions of the human spirit.

Though mystery enwraps the holy of holies, he would not choose other than his manhood, in spite of its sin and suffering. He can feel the helpful influence of his love and sorrow.

> I hold it true, whate'er befall;
>   I feel it when I sorrow most;
>   'Tis better to have loved and lost
> Than never to have loved at all.

It opens the avenues of his life and makes him more human.

> The shade by which my life was crost,
>   Which makes a desert in my mind,
>   Has made me kindly with my kind,
> And like to him whose light is lost.

Though the sight of man is dim and he cannot follow his friend, he cannot think of him as dead. He is ever present in waking thoughts and dreams of the night. His very grief is a measure of his friend's greatness, and somewhere that greatness must be doing its work. However sad and unanswerable the mystery of death, he will cherish his love, and will sing his song.

The *second cycle,* 78-104, shows the influence of time upon sorrow, the gradual lifting of the mists, so that some glory falls upon the world, and the pleasures of nature blend with the deeper voices of the soul.

He longs to see his friend with bodily eyes. This he knows cannot be granted; it must be a vision of the spirit. And the vision of the spirit can only be given to the calm and pure spirit. And so the gradual change is indicated, of which Nature herself is the symbol. The anniversary of Hallam's death is not stormy as before, but calm and beautiful. When the soul is prepared in quietness, faith with new vigor drives back the coward doubts and in mystic vision

> The dead man touch'd me from the past,
> And all at once it seem'd at last
> The living soul was flash'd on mine.

To the poet, the vision is foretaste and prophecy of the life immortal.

The *last cycle*, 104-131, has a different tone. It turns from personal experience to the world's need and hope. From the opening lines:

> Long sleeps the summer in the seed;
> Run out your measured arcs, and lead
> The closing cycle rich in good,

it moves with calmer and steadier step to

> the crowning race
> Of those that eye to eye shall look
> On Knowledge: . . .

> For all we thought and loved and did,
> And hoped, and suffer'd is but seed
> Of what in them is flower and fruit.

Grief must not be cherished as the luxury of love. Overmuch grief must be silenced; it must make us wise, if our work is to be done and the happier day come. So Tennyson turns to society and human progress; he sings the Christ that is to be. How much Arthur would have done with his "heart-affluence in discursive talk," his "seraphic intellect and force to seize and throw the doubts of man," his "impassioned logic, which outran the hearer in its fiery course." If the world has lost so much, the poet must not fail to do his part.

> All these have been, and thee mine eyes
>   Have look'd on: if they look'd in vain,
>   My shame is greater who remain,
> Nor let thy wisdom make me wise.

The evolution of earth and man suggest immortality, the crowning work of time, else evolution itself is meaningless. Each life must be a type and force of this higher progress. Amidst the mighty cosmic forces, the one abiding thing is the spirit, and the life of the spirit is love. Not by effort of the understanding do we apprehend God, but by the love of the heart; and that's what St. John said. He who cries after God shall feel Him. The faith that clings to Arthur is the faith that worketh by love through human struggles and hopes, working out the divine plan of a nobler race.

The poet that invoked Immortal Love in the beginning of his song, sings at its close,

> Love is and was my Lord and King;

and the prayer-hymn rises as the meaning of the years:

> O living will that shalt endure
>   When all that seems shall suffer shock,
>   Rise in the spiritual rock,
> Flow thro' our deeds and make them pure,
>
> That we may lift from out of dust
>   A voice as unto him that hears,
>   A cry above the conquered years
> To one that with us works, and trust,

With faith that comes of self-control,
The truths that never can be proved
Until we close with all we loved,
And all we flow from, soul in soul.

There are three characteristics that give "In Memoriam" its message to the soul of our generation,—the wonderful realism of its psychology of sorrow, its fearless but reverent facing the mysteries around and beyond us, and the triumphant faith possible for a life that will trust and follow the motions of its spiritual nature.

Only a life that in some degree has suffered as Tennyson did can know how faithful he is to the faintest motions of the soul in sorrow. The life of the world that breaks in upon our states of grief like far-away noise, the worthlessness of the attempted comfort that loss is common, the something of standing "where he in English earth is laid," the "vain pretense" of Christmas cheer, the converse about the loved and lost, taking

the grasses of the grave,
And make them pipes whereon to blow,

the life that almost dies, "that dies not, but endures with pain," the firmer mind, slowly forming,

Treasuring the look it can not find,
The words that are not heard again;—

such pictures (and there are many others), are a mirror in which the mourner salutes his very soul.

Mr. Tennyson frankly acknowledged the difficulty that many earnest minds have over religious belief. He does not minimize or qualify the questionings of skep-

tical science. He is faithful in following truth though
it seem to contradict some of his cherished hopes, though
it lead from beaten path of men to untrod ways. He
has a true humility as the only attitude for the human
soul that knows the finite can by no means grasp the
infinite. This sincerity to the deepest depth makes the
power of Tennyson in dealing with earnest and questioning souls. "Wordsworth's attitude towards nature
was one that left science unregarded: the nature for
which Wordsworth stirred our feelings was nature as
known by simple observation and interpreted by religious and sympathetic intuition. But for Tennyson
the physical world is always the world as known to us
through physical science; the scientific view of it domi-
nates his thoughts about it; and his general acceptance
of this view is real and sincere, even when he utters the
intensest feeling of its inadequacy to satisfy our deepest
needs."

Professor Sidgwick speaks of the "unparalleled
combination of intensity of feeling with comprehensive-
ness of view and balance of judgment, shown in pre-
senting the deepest needs and perplexities of humanity."
Tennyson was troubled by the lavish profusion in the
natural world, the apparent waste of life, and by the
vast amount of sin and suffering in the world, and he
confessed that they seemed to militate against the idea
of the omnipotent and all-loving Father. "Yet God
is love," he would exclaim after one of these moods.
"We do not get this faith from nature or the world.
If we look at nature alone, full of perfection and imperfection, she tells us that God is disease, murder, rapine.
We get this faith from ourselves, from what is highest
within us, which recognizes that there is not one fruitless pang, just as there is not one lost good." He does

not meet the atheistic tendencies of modern science with more confident defiance, but by appeal to those high instincts, those "questionings of sense and outward things" which are the witness of the spiritual nature.

And this brings us to the last thought, the victory of his faith and how he saves faith for questioning souls. He wins victory for himself and so for other tempted souls by cherishing the love and trust and hope of his spiritual nature, by trying to keep his life free from worldliness, by patiently awaiting the unfoldings of God, by loyally doing and bearing what seems the will of God. He so trusts in eternal justice and love that a life in such an attitude will not be left in weakness and darkness.

Each realm of God has its own organs and methods of vision. The natural world is apprehended by the senses through observation. This is what men call knowledge. The spiritual world is apprehended by obedience, by love, by trust, and this is faith. There can be no real conflict between religion and science, faith and knowledge, if each will keep to its own sphere and method. "Let the scientific men stick to their science," he says one day in a friendly discussion with Froude and Tyndall, "and leave philosophy and religion to poets, philosophers, and theologians." To him faith was the "faculty of the soul which enabled him to grasp truths inaccessible to understanding and knowledge, the very truths which are required to give life its meaning and consecration," and he believed that the efficacy of faith depended upon the condition of the heart and the will. And so he taught that faith comes from self-control, that it has its source in reverence, that it is the protest of the heart against the "freezing reason's colder part."

We have but faith: we can not know,
  For knowledge is of things we see;
  And yet we trust it comes from Thee,
A beam in darkness: let it grow.

Let knowledge grow from more to more,
  But more of reverence in us dwell:
  That mind and soul, according well
May make one music as before,

But vaster.

No doubt "In Memoriam" has had a certain "dissolving" influence (to use the word of James Martineau) upon religious thought, that is, it has released it from the too tight propositions which have tried to define the Infinite. And in this process of release, some lives have pushed beyond the forms of faith and lost the faith itself. But they have not followed the spirit of Tennyson. "He has never for himself surrendered the traditional form of a devout faith, till he has seized its permanent spirit, and invested it with a purer glory; so has he saved it for others by making it fairer than they had dreamt. Among thousands of readers previously irresponsible to anything Divine he has created, or immeasurably intensified, the susceptibility of religious reverence." (Martineau.)

I found Him not in world or sun,
  Or eagle's wing, or insect's eye:
  Nor thro' the questions men may try,
The petty cobwebs we have spun:

If e'er when faith had fall'n asleep,
  I heard a voice "Believe no more,"
  And heard an ever-breaking shore
That tumbled in the godless deep;

A warmth within the heart would melt
The freezing reason's colder part,
And like a man in wrath the heart
Stood up and answered, 'I have felt.'

No, like a child in doubt and fear;
But that blind clamour made me wise;
Then was I as a child that cries,
But crying, knows his father near;

And what I am beheld again
What is, and no man understands;
And out of darkness came the hands
That reach through nature, moulding men.

CHAPTER VI

Browning's Interpretation of Love

CHAPTER VI

BROWNING'S INTERPRETATION OF LOVE

Cannon Farrar in a lecture in this country said that the study of Robert Browning was equivalent to a liberal education. And it is not hard to see why this may be true.

Browning was an omnivorous student, of all the great concerns of human interest, of the various fields of human thought, even more than Tennyson a profound student of man. For while there is always something insular and English about Tennyson, Mr. Browning is a man of the world, and is the first great exponent in English literature of the world-consciousness. So in studying Browning, one is brought into contact with many lands and times and persons. Such intercourse tends to a liberal culture.

Mr. Browning is essentially a thinker; he is an interpreter of life, a philosopher before he is a poet; using his poetic genius, his power of penetrative insight, to see into the life of things, to pluck out the heart of the mystery; and he does this with such fertility, and originality, and often difficulty of thought and expression as to quicken and develop any mind that will make his poetry a serious study. As Mr. Stedman says of "The Ring and the Book": "The thought, the vocabulary, the imagery, the wisdom, lavished upon this story, would equip a score of ordinary writers, and place them beyond danger of neglect."

And then Mr. Browning is essentially a religious philosopher, an ethical teacher more than a metaphysician. He is the poet of the soul. He traces the inner processes of a life, hunting motives to the darkest hiding-places, laying open the motions of the heart, revealing a man to himself, showing that "life's business is just the terrible choice," showing morality necessarily ever under the guise of warfare, God's training of a soul.

So the study of Browning means a truer knowledge of the soul, and a grasp after the relation of man to the world and to God, beside the training of a wide culture. In his journey to Australia, Henry Drummond took a complete set of Browning, and recorded in his journal, "None can approach Browning in insight into life, or even into Christianity."

No man has come so slowly to his kingdom as Browning. Like Tennyson his father was a poet, though of little achievement, and the boy was trained to be a poet from childhood. As a little boy of eight he walked around the dining-room table, spanning out the scansion of his verses with his hand on the smooth mahogany. As early as this he debated between poetry and painting as a life work, but he didn't debate long, for it was only a moment's wavering of the purpose that controlled his conscious life, as he himself puts it thirty-five years after:

> I shall never in the years remaining,
> Paint you pictures, no, nor carve you statues,
> Make you music that should all-express me:
> Verse alone, one life allows me.

At twelve, he had poems enough for a volume, but tried in vain to get a publisher. Thus far he had been under the influence of Byron, and thought that feeling was the substance of poetry. But at thirteen, he found a mutilated copy of Shelley and soon was made passing rich with complete copies of Shelley and Keats, both poets dead and practically unknown to the British public. Then he began that training for a poet, in school and university, and in the wider school of life, by travel and study in many lands, in intercourse with many minds, that gave him something of Shakspere's universality. At twenty, he published "Pauline" anonymously. That was 1833, the year after Tennyson's second volume; but the poem was never acknowledged until 1867. Not a single copy was sold. The reviews ignored it or spoke contemptuously. Here and there a man like John Stuart Mill and John Forster and D. G. Rossetti read it and felt that a great soul was struggling for a voice. The next year four poems appeared in magazines, chief of them "Porphyria's Lover," and attracted no attention. A few copies of "Paracelsus" (1835), were sold but the reviews were still adverse. "Obscurity of Shelley minus his poetic beauty." Though Browning was gaining no public, he was making friends. Wordsworth hailed him as a brother poet. Macready the actor urged him to write for the stage, and in answer appeared the play of Strafford in 1837. "Pippa Passes" and "The Return of the Druses" were first written for the stage but found neither actor nor publisher. However, the masculine mind of Mr. Browning was not disheartened by apparent failure. He returned to his early plan of chronicling in poetry the whole life of a soul, and "Sordello" was the outcome, appearing in 1840, a poem that has been "an eminent stumbling-block, not merely in the path of fools, but in that of very sensible and cultivated people." Mr. Gosse admits that it needs reading three times, but declares that "on a third, even a school-boy of tolerable intelligence will find it luminous, if not entirely lucid."

All the books thus far had been published at the expense of his father, and at added financial loss.

From 1841 to 1846, under the general title of "Bells and Pomegranates," cheap sheets of his poems were printed that first found anything like a reading public. "Pippa Passes" was the first that in any sense became popular. In this series is such variety as "My Last Duchess," "In a Gondola," "A Blot on the 'Scutcheon," "A Soul's Tragedy," "Evelyn Hope," "Colombe's Birthday," "The Pied Piper." These are poems of lyric sweetness or fire, and others where the most exquisite charm and variety of music are fused with dramatic intensity. The incidents of outer action or the movements of the inner life of the soul are treated with ideality and harmony. The thought is in the highest sense poetic. This finished the first period of Mr. Browning's development.

Though most of Mr. Browning's poems have the dramatic spirit, they are not many of them dramatic in form. There is no real acting and no real conversations, but the thought is developed by a series of monologues. "I have ventured to display somewhat minutely the mood itself in its rise and progress, and have suffered the agency by which it is influenced and determined, to be generally discernible in its effects alone, and subordinate throughout, if not altogether excluded." This was Browning's true work, and after 1846, the publication of his last drama, he gave himself to lyrics and dramatic monologues. From 1846 to 1864 might be called the second and best period of his work. It covers almost two decades of the poet's life, from his thirty-fourth to his fifty-second year, when a man's life is usually at the fullest. And the two volumes published during this period, "Men and Women" and "Dramatis Personæ," contain the happiest and most varied expression of his power and are the culmination of his genius.

"Andrea del Sarto," "The Bishop Orders his Tomb," "In a Balcony," "James Lee's Wife," "Abt Vogler," "Rabbi Ben Ezra," "A Death in the Desert," "Prospice," are the most significant of this collection, "that unfold a thought, and by this very thought, reveal a character." In some cases, as "Rabbi Ben Ezra," the thought is the chief thing and the character only hinted. In others, as "The Bishop Orders his Tomb," the character is prominent and the thought is in the background.

This also is the period of Mr. Browning's married life. And one cannot doubt that the perfection of his work is due in part to the influence of Elizabeth Barrett Browning, who unquestionably is the first woman poet of the English language. Though her father never forgave Mr. Browning for carrying off his daughter, the marriage was a union of souls, a blessing in giving the world an example of pure wedded love and in developing two souls by a holy affection and so elevating their work and enriching our poetry.

It is not only the time when lyric love shines the sweetest and purest, but when the spiritual insight into the truths of the soul and of God in his world of nature and of man has its most unerring expression. Mrs. Browning was his good star.

All that I know
Of a certain star

Is, it can throw
(Like the angled spar)
Now a dart of red,
Now a dart of blue;
Till my friends have said
They would fain see, too,
My star that dartles the red and the blue!
Then it stops like a bird; like a flower, hangs furled:
They must solace themselves with the Saturn above it,
What matter to me if their star is a world?
Mine has opened its soul to me; therefore I love it.

"The Ring and the Book," published in 1868, may be called the turning-point in the poet's career. It is the longest and greatest of his creative works (some do not hesitate to say the greatest creative work since Shakspere); it is the culmination of his earlier and better tendencies and also contains indications of a change that made his remaining work more metaphysical and obscure, more diffuse and inartistic.

The volume of Mr. Browning's work since 1870 is greater than that of his literary activity for the thirty-five preceding years, but there is a distinct loss in poetic qualities. He has always appealed to intellect rather than feeling, but as the years went on the poet was less, the thinker was more. He had the same intellectual keenness, the wisdom of a lengthening experience, but the creative imagination, the power to give life and beauty to his thought slowly passed away, or at least was not used.

It has been said that Browning was long in coming to his kingdom, and we are not so sure as to what his kingdom is. He began his career with Tennyson and they passed close together into the realms of light. Browning has left a greater body of work than Tennyson, but how much will escape the tooth of time; who can tell. When Tennyson was made Laureate, Browning was hardly known beyond the circle of a few friends. On the first publication of "Pauline" not a single copy was ever sold. A few years ago the Boston Browning Society sent an order to London to bid four hundred dollars for a copy to be sold at auction, and failed to get it because the book brought twice that sum.

Men differ still very widely about Browning. Some are offended by his originality and declare it carelessness or eccentricity, an offense to clear thought and poetic taste. Others are stimulated to closer thought by the very difficulties he presents. The two attitudes are expressed by the two brothers Frederick and Alfred Tennyson, both poets and both intimate friends of Browning. The former said: "Though I have the highest esteem for Browning, and believe him to be a man of infinite learning, jest and bonhomie, and moreover a sterling heart that reverbs no hollowness, I verily believe his school of poetry to be the most grotesque conceivable. With the exception of the 'Blot on the 'Scutcheon,' through which you may possibly grope your way without the aid of an Ariadne, the rest appear to me to be Chinese puzzles, trackless labyrinths, unapproachable nebulosities." While Alfred Tennyson voices the mind of poets certainly when he says, "Browning never greatly cares about the glory of words or beauty of form. As for his obscurity in his great imaginative analyses, I believe it is a mistake to explain poetry too much; people have really a pleasure in discovering their own interpretations. He has a mighty intellect, but sometimes I can not read him. He seldom attempts the marriage of sense with sound, although he shows a spontaneous felicity in the adaptation of words

to ideas and feelings. I wish I had written his two
lines:

> "The little more and how much it is,
> The little less and what worlds away";

and again he speaks of him as the "greatest brained poet
in England."

Mr. Browning was a most genial and attractive personality. In youth he looked like a poet,—you have
seen engravings after the painting by Watts,—but in
the fulness of age more like a wise practical man of
affairs. It may be that he has drawn a portrait of
himself in "How It Strikes a Contemporary" in the
poet who has no airs, no picturesque costume, nothing
of the melodramatic, but who notes everything about
him, remembers everything, and can, if needed, tell
the tale, a Chaucer brought into the subtle and complex
life of modern civilization.

"It cannot have escaped the notice of anyone who
knew Robert Browning well, and who compares him
in thought with other men of genius whom he may have
known, that it was not his strength only, his vehement
and ever-eruptive force that distinguished him, but to
an almost equal extent his humanity. Of all great poets
he was the most accessible. To him the whole world
was full of vague possibilities of friendship. . . . And,
to those who shared a nearer intimacy than genial
acquaintanceship could offer, is there one left to-day
who was disappointed in his Browning or had any deep
fault to find with him as a friend? Surely, no! He
was human to the core, red with the warm blood to
the center of his being."

And this is the first thing you feel in reading his
poetry. And this is the truth he is always writing about,

the heart. There isn't a line that is mawkish and sentimental. He has a robust, masculine intellect and he
compels you to think before you have a right to feel.
He analyzes and dissects and follows coolly and crit-
ically the ways of the soul, but it is the way of feeling,
for that's the way with the soul. He anticipates much
that the psychologists have to tell us as to how our soul
proceeds. He largely deals with the tragic elements of
life. The peculiar, crucial tests of life, the situations
that unconsciously reveal the inmost action, the morbid
states, the individual developments all have a fascination for his intellect, and each is given with its own
color and form. There is only here and there a bit
that in a strict sense can be called personal to himself,
and yet you feel the broad, comprehensive, genial humanity of Browning, his great heart feeling with men
in the strange and fateful vicissitudes of their lives.
"It must be ten years ago, but the impression of the
incident is as fresh upon me as though it happened
yesterday," says Mr. Gosse, "that Mr. Browning passed
from languid and rather ineffectual discussion of some
persons well known to us both into vivid and passionate
apology for an act of his own Colombe."

Browning is like a great deep. It is easy to get
beyond one's depth or be blown out of sight of familiar
landmarks. But one thing even a slight student of
Browning must know, that the poet treats of the primal
passion of the heart. He is the poet of the soul and the
first thing he interprets is *love*. He couldn't be the interpreter of man and fail to do this; for love is the
elemental and universal passion. In the "Potter's
Wheel," Ian Maclaren has this fine interpretation: "It
has been said that each one of us could write one
romance out of his own experiences, and if that be true,

the subject would be love. Concerning this passion no self-respecting person will say much, and he that has felt its tides at their fullest will say least; but beyond question it remains the most irresistible and effectual in human experiences. In the second part of the Holy Scripture it is hardly touched upon, because the New Testament is the history of a cause; in the former part it meets us everywhere, from the idyll of Jacob and Rachel to the lamentable tragedy of Hosea, because the Old Testament is the story of human lives. The glory of pure love is sung in the Canticles; the pollution of unchaste love is declared in Proverbs. The romance of Isaac meeting Rebecca in the eventide, and being her true husband till death, is an eternal contrast to David's wandering passions and loathly degradation. Outside the Bible creative literature dealing with many motives has ever returned to love, and lavished its art on the analysis of this supreme passion, which, if bound with many cords, will yet tear itself free, and being outraged, will in the end pull down the very pillars of a human life. It may not be possible so to appraise the gains of life as to array them on a scale from highest to lowest, giving to culture, happiness, wealth, power, honor, each its own fixed place, since what is fascinating to one man is indifferent to his neighbor. No one in his senses can doubt, however, that love is the chief possession within our imagination, and that its power has not failed. For its sake a man has agonized and striven with the world and his soul; for its sake a woman has welcomed hardship and isolation, and both were right. Browning never struck a deeper and truer note than the divinity and sovereignty of love."

What does Browning mean by love? His love must never be confounded with lust, "hell's own blue tint."

It touches the physical life and in its roots no doubt reaches down to the animal world below us.   But it is infinitely more than natural, always mixed with the spirit.   A man must love or lust and here is the possible height or depth of the human soul.

Love in Browning is the "consecration of the undivided self."   It is infinite giving, holding nothing back. "A Woman's Last Word" gives the conception:

> Be a god and hold me
>   With a charm!
> Be a man and fold me
>   With thine arm!
>
> Teach me, only teach, Love!
>   As I ought
> I will speak thy speech, Love,
>   Think thy thought—
>
> Meet, if thou require it,
>   Both demands,
> Laying flesh and spirit
>   In thy hands.

Love joins life to life: they become under the unifying power of love like one soul.   They are joined together as Tennyson says, "like perfect music unto perfect words."   Tennyson always thinks of love as obedient to law, as a question of social order; but Browning's follows the high prompts of inner impulses.   The one thinks of the sacredness of the social bond: the other thinks of the divine power that works in human hearts bringing them into vital union with others for the perfecting of life.   So to Tennyson, going aside from well-marked lines is the sin of love,—transgression;—but to Browning it is omission:

The sin I impute to each frustrate ghost
Is, the unlit lamp and the ungirt loin;
Tho' the end in sight was a vice, I say.

The true union of heart and mind is the joy and good
of this earthly life: their alienation and separation make
the most pitiful chapter of human experience. It is
the pathos of "James Lee's Wife." We see the prize
of love as it slips despairingly out of reach.

I

Is all our fire of shipwreck wood,
  Oak and pine?
Oh, for the ills half-understood,
  The dim dead woe
  Long ago
Befallen this bitter coast of France!
Well, poor sailors took their chance;
  I take mine.

II

A ruddy shaft our fire must shoot
  O'er the sea:
Do sailors eye the casement—mute
  Drenched and stark,
  From their bark—
And envy, gnash their teeth for hate
O' the warm safe house and happy freight
  —Thee and me?

III

God help you, sailors, at your need!
  Spare the curse!

For some ships, safe in port indeed,
  Rot and rust,
  Run to dust,
All through worms i' the wood, which crept,
Gnawed our hearts out while we slept:
  That is worse.

IV

Who lived here before us two?
  Old-world pairs.
Did a woman ever—would I knew!—
  Watch the man
  With whom began
Love's voyage full-sail,—(now, gnash your
    teeth!)
When planks start, open hell beneath
  Unawares?

                ("By the Fireside")

Love is the power of new life: it speaks to latent
powers and calls them forth: it is the motive for high
endeavor, the source of heroism and goodness. The
main question is, Has a life learned to love another?
it is the beginning of a higher life.

One made to love you, let the world take note!
Have I done worthy work? be love's the praise,
Tho' hampered by restrictions, barred against
By set forms, blinded by forced secrecies!
Set free my love, and see what love can do
Shown in my life—what work will spring from that!
The world is used to have its business done
On other grounds, find great effects produced
For power's sake, fame's sake, motives in men's mouth!
So, good: but let my low ground shame their high!
Truth is the strong thing. Let man's life be true!
And love's the truth of mine.

                ("In a Balcony")

True love always strives to purify and enrich. Love is of God and the very act has in it that which impels the soul homeward.

> Let her but love you,
> All else you disregard! What else can be?
> You know how love is incompatible
> With falsehood—purifies, assimilates
> All other passions to itself.
>   ("Colombe's Birthday")

> Ne'er wrong yourself so far as quote the world
> And say, love can go unrequited here!
> You will have blessed him to his whole life's end—
> Low passions hindered, baser cares kept back,
> All goodness cherished where you dwelt,—and dwell.

Browning holds that love has in itself this purifying and ennobling power, however evil it be circumstanced, and however evil be its beginning. However we must remember that it must be love, some soul mixed with it, and not mere fleshly passion. If a spark of genuine love kindle in the heart of an impure life, it will tend, just so far as it is suffered to work, to cleanse the old baseness.

> What is wanting to success,
> If somehow every face, no matter how deform,
> Evidence, to some one of hearts on earth, that, warm
> Beneath the veriest ash, there hides a spark of soul
> Which, quickened by love's breath, may yet pervade
>   the whole
> O' the gray, and, free again, be fire?—of worth the
>   same,
> Howe'er produced, for, great or little, flame is flame.
>   ("Fifine," xliii)

Though there is this element of divineness in true love, that tends to lift life to better things, its power is best seen in a pure life, in a Pamphilia or a Caponsacchi, it then shows likest God, for then only it has freedom to work. Like mercy or any other noble grace, it is mightiest in the mighty. In such lives it is felt to be an incoming of the heavenly life.

> God never is dishonored in the spark
> He gave us from his fire of fires, and bade
> Remember whence it sprang, nor be afraid
> While that burns on, tho' all the rest grow dim.
> ("Any Wife to Any Husband")

While love is the supreme object of man (no man is wholly without it, Nature herself has hints and foregleams of it, the roots of love and sacrifice reach down to the lowest nook and cranny of the world), the failure to realize the union of life with life, of soul with soul, what Plato called "the perfect whole," makes the real suffering and pathos and tragedy of life.

Even the base Ottima in "Pippa Passes" feels the beginning of terrible desolation as the gross love of herself and Sebald are flashed upon their souls in the song of the pure Pippa, and in the guilty man lust is turned to hate.

> That little peasant's voice
> Has righted all again. Though I be lost,
> I know which is the better, never fear,
> Of vice or virtue, purity or lust,
> Nature or trick! I see what I have done,
> Entirely now! Oh I am proud to feel
> Such torments—let the world take credit thence—
> I, having done my deed, pay too its price!
> I hate, hate—curse you! God's in his heaven!

"Two in the Campagna" traces the infinite passion and the pain of finite hearts that yearn, and yet one refuses to learn the lesson of nature.

> I would that you were all to me,
> You that are just so much, no more.
> Nor yours nor mine, nor slave nor free!
> Where does the fault lie? What the core
> O' the wound, since wound must be?

In "The Worst of It," the wronged one cannot forget love and so the soul is purified:

> Well, it is lost now; well, you must bear,
> Abide and grow fit for a better day:
> You should hardly grudge, could I be your judge!
> But trust! For you, can be no despair:
> There's amends: 'tis a secret: hope and pray!

. Enough has been said to show the lofty spiritual conception of Browning's idea of love. One must keep this in mind to be saved from the sensual interpretation of some of his poems. The expression of this love is oftentimes irregular, contrary to the seeming laws of society and God, a mere unguided impulse fed from below rather than above, but Browning does not mean it so, and if it have that impression on us it is because we carry into it our own evil desires. Here surely it is true that to the pure all things are pure. Sir Henry Jones in interpreting this truth of Browning declares, "Love is no accident in man's history nor a passing emotion. It is rather a constitutive element of man's nature, fundamental and necessary as his intelligence. It is the constructive power that has built the world of morality, binding man to man and age to age." It may be a long way from mere sex-passion, seen in the animals, to religious aspiration and self-surrender to God, but love is in all the moral and spiritual growth of men. It is not simply passion nor affection: it is intuition and ecstasy, and spiritual vision and eternal ideals. Love is man's moral ideal and therefore is the very gift of God. So it is the key to the enigmas of life, the supreme moral motive, the veritable nature of both God and man. Love is of God, and he that loveth knoweth God. "It is the revelation of the Infinite Love to our souls which makes any worthy love of woman for man, or man for woman."

So love is the supreme motive of Browning's art; he is always strong when dealing with it, and tries to reduce all phenomena of human experience to this single principle. Others have given love more tenderness and grace; none have given it such sweep and development. He has given to love its moral significance because the soul is to Browning the supreme thing and he always treats its love with spiritual earnestness.

From Browning's doctrine of love comes his optimism, and he is the great optimist among poets. He wouldn't be Browning without it.

No doubt Browning was an optimist by temperament. From his early years, we know that he had discipline and many things to wound a sensitive spirit. But he did not dwell in the shadows. He walked in the sun. He kept a child's delight in all simple pleasures, while his nature was responsive to all the good gifts of life. He had exuberant health and a buoyant nature and unfeigned humanity. The world seemed very good to him. The earth was a fit home for man.

Earth's changes, losses, struggles, did not change his temper. He had the habit of looking on the bright

side. "At the 'Mermaid'" gives the hopeful spirit of
Mr. Browning's disposition:

> Have you found your life distasteful?
>   My life did and does smack sweet.
> Was your youth of pleasure wasteful?
>   Mine I saved and hold complete.
> Do your joys with age diminish?
>   When mine fail me, I'll complain.
> Must in death your daylight finish?
>   My sun sets to rise again.

But Mr. Browning's optimism was more than a matter of health and sentiment. It was a profound conviction. Life was organic; man belonged to a moral
order, and that meant a harmonious world. It was not
so now. The moral world was in a process of building.
Human life was slowly and painfully realizing its ideal.
But the warring elements were a prophecy of the world
to be. The conviction of this purpose and process, of
this final harmony of self and the world and God came
from his doctrine of love.

It was not an easy faith. He had to fight his way
to it, even as Childe Roland to the Dark Tower came.
He would not make his judgment blind. He would face
all the facts of life. He has as religious a purpose as
Milton in "Paradise Lost." He would justify the ways
of God to man. Browning tries to give a philosophy
of life. If love rules, it must issue in complete moral
order.

> So, gazing up, in my youth, at love
> As seen thro' powers, ever above
> All modes which make it manifest,
> My soul brought all to a single test—

That He, the eternal first and last,
Who in his power had so surpassed
All man conceives of what is might,—
Whose wisdom, too, showed infinite,
   Would prove us infinitely good:
Would never (my soul understood)
With power to work all love desires,
Bestow e'en less than man requires.

("Christmas Eve")

Browning thinks of God as immanent, man's love as the expression of the Divine love.

Love which, on earth, amid all the shows of it,
Has ever been seen the sole good of life in it,
The love, ever growing there, spite of the strife in it,
   Shall arise, made perfect, from Death's repose of it;
And I shall behold Thee, face to face,
O God, and in Thy light retrace
How in all I loved here, still was't Thou.

("Christmas Eve")

But Browning is not satisfied to admit, to feel the power of love. He would make all things plain. The poet turns philosopher.

Remember, he holds to a moral order, that love is the law of the moral order, that love in man is the spark of God, that God is working through love for the redemption of the world.

Now the poet faces a prudential difficulty. The doctrine of love is bruised against the hard facts of life, its sins and miseries and failures. Love itself seems prostituted. The divine fire is gone: nothing left but cold gray ashes. How can you say that "all's love, yet all's law," when you see evil? Browning answers. How do you know that it is absolute evil? It

may be only a foil to the good, only a means by which
the soul is developed.

> As night needs day, as shine needs shade, so good
> Needs evil: how were pity understood
> Unless by pain.

Here comes the doctrine of the relativity of knowledge, and he pushes it so far that a less robust faith
might easily fall into agnosticism. He draws the same
antithesis between knowledge and love that Tennyson
does between knowledge and faith.

But reason will say to this philosophy of doubt, If
you mistrust the conclusions of knowledge, how do you
know that love itself is of God and to be trusted? And
here Browning appeals from reason to conscience.
What does the heart, the moral consciousness, say?
Whatever the uses of evil, we know the fact of evil.
We know it as evil: we have tasted its bitter fruit. The
very evil in our hearts begets divine discontent and the
undying hope of something better:

> Then life is—to wake not sleep,
> Rise and not rest, but press
> From earth's level, where blindly creep
> Things perfected, more or less,
> To the heaven's bright, far steep,
> Where, amid what strifes and storms
> May wait the adventurous quest,
> Power is love—transports, transforms.
> Who aspired from worst to best,
> Sought the soul's world, spurned the worms.

Browning tries to harmonize all facts with his
philosophy of love. As life is a growth, it is not possible

at any time to pass fixed judgments upon man's action. We grow by contest. To have contest we must recognize evil as evil, and as such hate and fight it. It may be only imperfect good. It is love's way of progress. You see the poet assumes or denies the possibility of knowledge as it suits his philosophy. We may deny our knowledge of evil: we build on our knowledge of love.

Life is not so simple as that. We would better stand with uncovered heads in the presence of God, and the mystery of evil. The first fallacy is the denial that God works through intelligence, but does work through love; and the second that our knowledge of sin is an illusion.

We turn from Browning the philosopher to Browning the poet. Whatever the mazes of his philosophy, his spiritual instincts and visions never grow old. "Long as he lived, he did not live long enough for one of his ideals to vanish, for one of his enthusiasms to lose its heat."

There shall never be one lost good! . . .
All we have willed or hoped or dreamed of good shall
        exist;
Not its semblance, but itself: no beauty, nor good, nor
        power
Whose voice has gone forth, but each survives for the
        melodist,
When eternity affirms the conception of an hour.

                            ("Abt Vogler")

There is no better tonic for anæmic Christianity than the poetry of Browning. It is God's message to an age whose intellectual life is often marked by a cynical pessimism. It is the noblest food of the soul for young

men who aspire to be spiritual leaders, who need vision
and faith and courage. He was

One who never turned his back, but marched breast
      forward,
Never doubted clouds would break,
Never dreamed, though right were worsted, wrong would
      triumph,
Held we fall to rise, are baffled to fight better,
    Sleep to wake.

                            ("Asolando")

CHAPTER VII

Browning's Interpretation of the Incarnation

CHAPTER VII

BROWNING'S INTERPRETATION OF THE INCARNATION

Mr. Browning was a thoroughgoing idealist. On the solid English earth, his mind was above the mists and the malaria of a too practical earthly life. His shrewd, kindly, human eyes saw the passing show of life, noted every transient form and grace; but ever tried to penetrate to their deeper meaning. He was a humanist, friendly to all humankind, but the ladder of life did not lie flat along the earth, but rose to the heavens. He tried to measure the movement of mankind, to understand the purpose and the goal of human life.

> Like a poet hidden
> In the light of thought,
> Singing hymns unbidden,
> Till the world is wrought
> To sympathy with hopes and fears it heeded not.

In four ways Mr. Browning is ever showing his idealism. (1) The importance of the inner and spiritual life over the outer and material. (2) The sense of a personal God in all the life of the world, not to be demonstrated but accepted as one's own life, without whom life is unaccountable and the world a ship of fools. (3) This world the vestibule of the eternal, immortality an inevitable inference from the fact of God and man's relation to God.

> All that is, at all,
> Lasts ever, past recall;
> Earth changes, but thy soul and God stand sure:
> What entered into thee,
> That was, is, and shall be:
> Time's wheel runs back or stops: Potter and clay
>   endure.

(4) And therefore the significance of life is in its *growth*. Whatever checks, dwarfs the life is evil; whatever contributes to the freedom, fulness, growth of life is good, is God's way of training a soul. And so to Browning, life is tested by its desire and struggle.

> Ah! but a man's reach should exceed his grasp,
> Or what's a heaven for?

Real life is positive, not negative, a passion for the higher. It is violence that taketh the kingdom of heaven. The sin of life is inaction and low content, "the unlit lamp, and the ungirt loin."

And here we have the key to Browning's interpretation of the Incarnation. God reveals Himself in Christ not simply to overcome evil, to forgive a man's sin and purge it away, so that life shall be free from defect. Sin is not the great fact. It is an obstacle, an incident, "a silence signifying sound," a thing to be resisted that strength may be gained, to be fought that the warrior may be crowned. The center of all is man's life, and that means man's growth. And the Incarnation is needed for the revelation, and freedom and joy and growth of a man's life. The Incarnation, to Browning, is God's way of making a man.

I

Take first, the *Demand* for the *Incarnation*. (A) The growth of life, the progress of man, demands the revelation of God to show the meaning of each life and the goal of growth. As man is a living soul, a self-directing, responsible life, the ideal of this life must be ever before him if a true growth is to be attained, to make the way plain. "Cleon" is the cry of the human heart for a manifest God. There must be some purpose in all the work of life beyond the work itself. Cleon, the Greek poet from whom Paul quotes in his speech on Mars Hill, draws this lesson from the work of the king to whom he writes:

> Thou, in the daily building of thy tower,
> Whether in fierce and sudden spasms of toil,
> Or thro' dim lulls of unapparent growth,
> Or when the general work 'mid good acclaim
> Climbed with the eye to cheer the architect,
> Did'st ne'er engage in work for mere work's sake—
> Had'st ever in thy heart the luring hope
> Of some eventual rest a-top of it,
> Whence, all the tumult of the building hushed,
> Thou first of men might'st look out to the East:
> The vulgar saw thy tower; thou sawest the sun.

And so of his own work, Cleon says. He had been a great artist and wrought well.

> All arts are mine;
> Thus much the people know and recognize,
> Throughout our seventeen isles.

And he is only one of a long line of workers. He tries
to compare his work with that of his forerunners.
With greater mind, he still looks not so great beside
their simple way. But how can one judge a certain part
when each part has reference to all? How can we
know this sequence of the soul's achievement here?

> Mankind, made up of all the single men,—
> In such a synthesis the labor ends.

Is there true growth? Is there some ideal towards
which the whole building is rising? How can we know
its meaning?

> And thus our soul, misknown, cries out to Zeus
> To vindicate his purpose in our life:
> Why stay we on the earth unless to grow?
> Long since, I imaged, wrote the fiction out,
> That he or other god descended here
> And, once for all, showed simultaneously
> What, in its nature, never can be shown
> Piecemeal or in succession;—showed, I say,
> The worth both absolute and relative
> Of all his children from the birth of time,
> His instruments for all appointed work.

Is this vision of God coming into human life to show
its meaning, to point out its goal, only the dream of a
poet? It is no dream,

> That years and days, the summers and the springs,
> Follow each other with unwaning powers.
> The grapes which dye thy wine are richer far
> Through culture than the wild wealth of the rock;
> The pastured honey-bee drops choicer sweet;
> The flowers turn double, and the leaves turn flowers.

This is no dream. This is a matter of experience. We can see the growth of nature. We can trace the development through her various forms of life. This is a presumptive argument for the growth and fuller development of human life. What we see must be the beginning of an infinite growth. All lower life develops and—man!

What! and the soul alone deteriorates?

This is the argument of hope, but the heart cries out then as ever, "Show us the Father and it sufficeth us." We long to have God descend to show the worth of all his children. So the experience of man demands a fuller revelation to tell us the meaning and issue of life. This is the demand for the Incarnation.

(B) But we see the progress of life here. Man leaves the low levels of the natural life, the brute life, and gains the higher levels of the mind, the noble achievements of the civilized life. Why is not this enough, what we can see and gain here? Why not be content with our limits? The answer of Cleon is that the progress and achievement of man is a mockery without the life beyond. Is there a future life? No man from reason can surely say.

It needs a spirit glance in realms beyond the sun.

This is the demand for the Incarnation, a life that manifests and proves a higher realm than man of himself can know.

(1) Unless we have the future life, progress itself will be in vain. Shall we suffer and struggle and achieve, "gain ground upon the whole," have the vision

and hope of something better,—only to be snuffed out as a candle, to die like the brute? Better the contentment of the beast than to have attained so much and hoped for so much, and then the end!

> Let progress end at once,—man make no step
> Beyond the natural man, the better beast,
> Using his senses, not the sense of sense.
> In man there's failure, only since he left
> The lower and inconscious forms of life.
> We called it an advance, the rendering plain
> Man's spirit might grow conscious of man's life,
> And, by new love so added to the old,
> Take each step higher over the brute's head.
> This grew the only life, the pleasure-house,
> Watch tower and treasure-fortress of the soul,
> Which whole surrounding flats of natural life
> Seemed only fit to yield subsistence to;
> A tower that crowns a country,—But alas,
> *The soul now climbs it just to perish there!*

The poet asks the reason for all this seeming defeat of man.

> A man can use but a man's joy
> While he sees God's.

It cannot be the malice of God. He will not suffer himself to think that.

> Is it carelessness?
> Still, no. If care—where is the sign, I ask,
> And yet no answer, and agree in sum,
> O King, with thy profound discouragement,
> Who seest the wider, but to sigh the more,
> Most progress is most failure; thou sayest well.

That's what Paul said; "If in this life only we have hoped, we are of all men most pitiable." The great motives and forces of human progress would be weakened without the hope of the future.

(2) But to return to Cleon's argument. If the personal life of man beyond these earthly limits is uncertain, not so his work and influence. That shall live on in the race: that is our contribution to the development of mankind. "Why should we have two immortalities," said the old skeptics,—as the new ones also say. Is not this craving for the continuance of the personal life a kind of selfishness? We can all join George Eliot's "Choir Invisible."

> May I reach
> That purest heaven, be to other souls
> The cup of strength in some great agony,
> Enkindle generous ardor, feed pure love,
> Beget the smiles that have no cruelty—
> Be the sweet presence of a good diffused,
> And in diffusion ever more intense.
> So shall I join the choir invisible
> Whose music is the gladness of the world.

But unconscious immortality will never satisfy a man. If this life is all, the practical conclusion will be that the sensualist or the pessimist has the best of it. It is a question whether all this struggle and sorrow is worth the candle. Joy demands a larger, freer air in which to live and breathe. Man's growth must be something more than a tower rising from the earth. He must do more than build his sepulchre. Not only the meaning and growth of life demand the revelation of a future world, but the very satisfaction of man, the sense of joy for which he was made, cannot be met without it.

Cleon is not comforted because the king speaks of the immortality of the poet's work.

What
Thou writest, paintest, stays; that does not die:
Sappho survives, because we sing her songs,
And Æschylus, because we read his plays!

*   *   *   *   *

Thou diest while I survive?
Say rather that my fate is deadlier still,
In this, that every day my sense of joy
Grows more acute, my soul (intensified
By power and insight) more enlarged, more keen;
While every day my hairs fall more and more,
My hand shakes, and the heavy years increase,—
My horror quickening still from year to year,
The consummation coming past escape,
When I shall know most, and yet least enjoy,—
When all my works wherein I prove my worth,
Being present still to mock me in men's mouths,
Alive still, in the phrase of such as thou,
I, I the feeling, thinking, acting man,
The man who loved his life so overmuch,
Shall sleep in my urn. It is so horrible,
I dare at times imagine to my need
Some future state revealed to us by Zeus,
Unlimited in capability
For joy, as this is in desire for joy,—
To seek which, the joy-hunger forces us:
That, stung by straitness of our life, made strait
On purpose to make prized the life at large—
Freed by the throbbing impulse we call death,
We burst there as the worm into the fly,
Who, while a worm still, wants his wings,—But no!
Zeus has not yet revealed it; and alas,
He must have done so, were it possible.

Thus Mr. Browning puts into the speech of Cleon that infinite pathos of the Old World shut up to the limit of this life; and as seen in more than one of the great thinkers and poets, a longing for fuller light. And at the same time, he makes him express the scorn which the cultivated Greek world would feel at being taught by a Jewish peasant.

> Thou canst not think a mere barbarian Jew,
> As Paulus proves to be, one circumcised,
> Hath access to a secret shut from us?

Christ was to the Greeks foolishness.

"*Cleon*" is the voice of reason, demanding the Incarnation to make life intelligible; "*Karshish*" is the instinctive cry of the heart to make life moral and beneficent. Karshish, an Arab physician, traveling in Palestine to gain knowledge for his work, chances to meet with Lazarus, and tells his strange story in a letter to Abib his master. It is one of the most characteristic and significant of Browning's dramatic monologues. Through all the calculated thought and plan of Karshish is revealed the deep impression made upon him by the man and his story. His very heart is laid bare as the impress of the early seas in the geologic strata. He tells the singular way in which he met the man. He recounts the story of his restoration from the grave.

> The man's own firm conviction rests
> That he was dead (in fact they buried him)
> —That he was dead and then restored to life
> By a Nazarene physician of his tribe.

The Arab calls it only a case of mania, superinduced by epilepsy. But in spite of this easy judgment, he admits

that the case has struck him far more than 'tis worth.
He admits that this man has a different attitude towards
life.

> Whence has the man the balm that brightens all?
> So here—we call the treasure knowledge, say,
> Increased beyond the fleshly faculty—
> Heaven opened to a soul while yet on earth,
> Earth forced on a soul's use while seeing heaven.

He wonders that men do not see with his opened eyes.

> Indeed, the special marking of the man
> Is pious submission to the heavenly will—
> Seeing it, what it is, and why it is.

Karshish admits this life so different from every other,
but of course a learned doctor must write,

> And, after all, our patient Lazarus
> Is stark mad.
> This man so cured regards the curer, then,
> As,—God forgive me! who but God himself,
> Creator and Sustainer of the world,
> That came and dwelt in flesh on it awhile!
> *   *   *   *   *
> Who saith—but why all this of what he saith?
> Why write of trivial matters, things of price
> Calling at every moment for remark?
> I noticed on the margin of a pool
> Blue-flowering borage, the Aleppo sort,
> Aboundeth, very nitrous.

Then the deep impression breaks through the careless
manner, and he adds, "It is strange!" And with another

brief reference to Lazarus, and then some more commonplaces, the physician's very heart, all the deep and even unconscious longings for that which he had never before been able to express, bursts forth in the postscript of the letter (among the noblest words of Browning).

> The very God! think, Abib; dost thou think?
> So, the All-great were the All-Loving too—
> So, through the thunder comes a human voice
> Saying, 'O heart, I made, a heart beats here!
> Face, my hands fashioned, see it in myself!
> Thou hast no power nor may'st conceive of mine,
> But love I gave thee, with myself to love,
> And thou must love me who have died for thee!'
> The madman saith He said so: it is strange.

This is the heart-cry that so many men have uttered from the drama of Job, with its "God is not a man as I am . . . Neither is there any daysman betwixt us to lay his hand upon us both"; to the words of Horace Bushness in our own day: "My heart cries out for God. I can shatter the doctrine of the Trinity with my reason, but my heart needs God the Father, and God the Son, and God the Holy Spirit."

Men know the power of God, if they admit the fact of God at all. But they stumble at the love of God. How can the All-great be the All-loving in this world of pain and moral disorder! If man has a nature that allies him to God, the heart of the child that cannot be content without the revelation of the heart of the Father is the strongest demand for the Incarnation. And this is the striking witness of Karshish.

II

The demand for Revelation is answered in Christ. Christ as the divine complement to man's need is taught by Browning especially in three poems: "The Ring and the Book," "Christmas Eve," and "Easter Day."

(A) "The Ring and the Book" is the longest and most difficult of the poems. Twelve books are written on a single tragic tale found in an old manuscript; the story as regarded by twelve different groups of people; their relation to it, their thoughts, their speech, their conduct, the very atmosphere of their lives, all revealing character: enough material, as one critic truly says, to make the reputation of a score of poets.

It is in "The Pope" that the *reasonableness* of the Incarnation is expressed. The doctrine meets the heart of man, but can it satisfy the reason? To have the heart rise up and say with Tennyson "I have felt," is not enough for the great conviction that shall control the race. Man is a unit and the intellect must give its assent to the promptings of the heart. The Incarnation is a question of the reason also: it must be met and answered there. Look at the Incarnation as the question of the mind. Man is the highest mind that we know here. But man fails of his own conceivable height, i.e., man's mind cannot account for the world. We must go to God. A life greater than ourselves must account for man, for all the process that has resulted in the mind of man.

We must judge God by his world. That's the law of knowledge. Beyond this we cannot go. And what does the world say of God? What do the works of God reveal? In them, we find *power* enough. In them,

we find *intelligence* ample. But goodness? Here the
revelation of God fails. Nature often seems "red in
tooth and claw with ravin." Human life often seems
a tangled skein. But the Incarnation throws light upon
it all. The Easter morn sheds a new glory on the
earth. Bethlehem and Calvary bring human life out of
the shadow. Pain is not so dark, its burden is certainly
lightened—when we know that God himself has entered
into it, "bearing our sins and carrying our sorrows."
The Incarnation makes *love* unlimited and complete.
Then reason is satisfied, there is perfection fit for God.
But let Browning express the thought. The Pope says:

> There is, beside the works, a tale of Thee
> In the world's mouth, which I find credible:
> I love it with my heart: unsatisfied,
> I try it with my reason, nor discept
> From any point I probe and pronounce sound.
> Mind is not matter, nor from matter, but
> Above,—leave matter, then, proceed with mind!
> Man's be the mind recognized at the height,—
> Leave the inferior minds and look at man!
> Is he the strong, intelligent, and good
> Up to his own conceivable height? Nowise.
> Enough o' the low,—soar the conceivable height,
> Find cause to match the effect in evidence,
> The work i' the world, not man's but God's; leave man!
> Conjecture of the worker by the work:
> Is there strength there?—enough: intelligence?
> Ample: but goodness in a like degree?
> Not to the human eye in the present state,
> An isosceles deficient in the base.
> What lacks, then, of perfection fit for God
> But just the instance which this tale supplies
> Of love without a limit? So is strength,
> So is intelligence; let love be so,

> Unlimited in its self-sacrifice,
> Then is the tale true and God shows complete.

Beyond this, Browning would say,

> I reach into the dark,
> Feel what I cannot see; and still faith stands.

Whether sin and suffering are for moral training here, not absolute evil, this is all surmise. The Incarnation is revealed and it meets the demands of reason.

(B) In "Christmas Eve," Browning impressively teaches that all who believe that God in Christ has given Himself in love to men, know God and have fellowship with Him. On Christmas Eve, the poet finds himself in a mean chapel in a mean neighborhood. No doubt it is a memory of his own youth in York St. chapel, South London, now the seat of the Browning Hall Settlement. The congregation seems repulsive to a man of taste and the preacher gives them the merest commonplaces of the Gospel. There was no suggestion to the poet of the deep things of God, and he goes out under the night sky where God seems nearer to him.

> In youth I looked to those very skies
> And, probing their immensities,
> I found God there, His visible *Power;*
> Yet felt in my heart, amid all its sense
> Of the Power, an equal evidence
> That His Love, there too, was the nobler dower;
> For the loving worm within the clod
> Were diviner than a loveless God
> Amid His worlds, I well dare to say.

The poet has a wonderful vision of the sky and seems to feel that some one will come forth from the very place of God. Then a blinding storm sweeps away the vision, and when the sky has cleared, the figure of Christ appears before him.

> He was there,
> He himself with the human air
> On the rainbow pathway, just before.

Christ's back is turned towards him, and then the poet understands that he has been in the despised chapel, with its poor folk. And Christ is grieved at his own blindness and disdain. He pleads with Christ that he had left the chapel because they had such narrow, unworthy ideas of Him, and had sought the open heaven that Christ in His real glory might appear. Then Christ turned his face upon him with such a glory that he could not bear it.

Swept along by the hem of Christ's robe, the poet suddenly finds himself at Rome, witnessing the splendid ceremonial of Christmas Eve at St. Peter's. He is offended at the grotesqueness and vainglory of the worship, but he has learned the lesson of the chapel and the vision, and that the elaborate ceremonial is the imperfect human way of trying to express the stupendous fact of the Incarnation.

Once more the scene changes and the poet is in a lecture room at Göttingen, listening to a learned Professor explaining the myth of Christ. He explains away all the mysterious in the person of Christ, makes him simply a good man. And the Professor ends his lecture by urging his students to cherish the tender and pathetic story of Christ's life and death, though they can no longer worship Him and place their hopes upon Him. The poet feels the chill of the critical class room, and knows that the learned Professor has not touched the hem of Christ's garment.

And here Browning shows his own deep faith in the Incarnation. In light, bantering satire,—but the poet is never more earnest,—he shows what reverencing the myth amounts to. Christ no longer supports us, but we try to support the Christ, try to draw light and comfort from the very creature which our own imagination has made.

> Deduce from this lecture all that eases you;
> Nay, call yourselves, if the calling pleases you,
> 'Christians',—abhor the deist's pravity—
> Go on, you shall no more move my gravity—
> Than, when I see boys ride a-cock horse
> I find it in my heart to embarrass them
> By hinting that their stick's a mock horse
> And they really carry what they say carries them.

Once more the poet is back at Zion chapel, where all the time he had been dreaming, and the poem closes with one of the noblest pleas of practical faith. Christ does meet the world's need; and what more can the mind of man ask!

> Is God mocked, as he asks?
> Shall I take on me to change His tasks,
> And dare, despatched to a river-head
> For a simple draught of the element,
> Neglect the thing for which he sent,
> And return with another thing instead?
> Saying, 'Because the water found
> Welling up from underground,

Is mingled with the taints of earth,
While thou, I know, dost laugh at dearth,
And could'st, at wink or word, convulse
The world with the leap of a river-pulse,—
Therefore I turn from the oozings muddy,
And bring thee a chalice I found instead:
See the brave veins in the breccia ruddy!
One would suppose, that the marble bled.
What matters the water? I hope I have nursed:
The waterless cup will quench my thirst.'
—Better have knelt at the poorest stream
That trickles in pain from the straitest rift!
For the less or the more is all God's gift,
Who blocks up or breaks wide the granite-seam.
And here, is there water or not to drink?
I then, in ignorance and weakness,
Taking God's help, have attained to think
My heart does best to receive in meekness
That mode of Worship, as most to his mind,
Where earthly aids being cast behind,
His All in All appears serene
With the thinnest human veil between,
Setting the mystic lamps, the seven,
The many motions of his Spirit,
Pass, as they list, from earth to heaven.
For the preacher's merit or demerit,
It were to be wished the flaws were fewer
In the earthen vessel holding treasure,
Which lies as safe as in a golden ewer;
But the main thing is, does it hold good measure?
Heaven soon sets right all other matter!

(C) In "Easter Day," Mr. Browning deals with the
practical difficulties of faith in the Incarnation. There
are speculative difficulties,—every honest thinker must
admit them,—but the practical difficulties of life are

what really stand in the way of faith. It is *hard* to be a Christian, is the gist of the trouble.

Belief stands first. A man must accept the fact of the Incarnation. It is not absolutely certain, says the critical mind. But some uncertainty is necessary to faith. It is so with our human affairs. About the matters that greatly concern us, we can never be absolutely certain, yet we are compelled to act, and it is the act of faith. But should it not be different with God in Christ? The fact is so stupendous and makes such radical demands upon us? Can't we demonstrate God? Can't we have exacter laws? No; the greatest truths never can be proved. A scientific faith is absurd. A man must act upon probability in all matters of moral conduct, and there is probability enough for the Christ. You'll find evidence, if you desire. There is historic fact and human need that interprets the fact.

But belief in Christ makes such demand upon us. The Christ is not simply to give our joys zest, to add a certain spiritual culture to men: he demands the great *renunciation*. Take up the Cross, and follow me. What if we should renounce life for death only? We have *hope* and by this we must live.

The real choice of life is presented through the vision of the Judgment and the figure of Christ.

The soul says the earth is too close and good to give up. Then, Heaven is lost, is the answer. If we must give up the pleasant life of earth as the chief good, then, says man, we will choose mind and its works. Surely the intellectual life is the higher life. And the answer of the Judge is,—still it is the choice of earth. There is one good left, pleads the soul, and that is human love. Choose love, then, for there can be nothing better than love. Blind, blind, replies the Christ. The

Divine Love is through earth, mind, love, to help men
make the true use of all. Christ, the Divine Love incarnate, must be seen and chosen, if the fair and noble
things of earth are to project the soul on its lone way.
And the words of Browning are the practical witness
of every life that bows before the wonderful vision of
the Christ.

> And I cowered deprecatingly—
> Thou Love of God! Or let me die,
> Or grant what shall seem heaven almost!
> Let me not know that all is lost,
> Though lost it be;—leave me not tied
> To this despair, this corpse-like bride!
> Let that old life seem mine—no more—
> With limitation as before,
> With darkness, hunger, toil, distress:
> Be all the earth a wilderness!
> Only let me go on, go on,
> Still hoping ever and anon
> To reach one eve the Better Land!

III

Thus far Browning's belief in the Incarnation has
been interpreted, his reasons for holding it, however
mysterious, as the great fact of life. It remains to
be seen how Browning realized the truth, so that it
became more than an infinite fact to be accepted by the
reason,—how it became the vital truth of his thought
and life. The method by which the poet would make
the Incarnation real to himself and to all men is seen in
the poem "Saul." It teaches that *Love Incarnate* is the
only *power to redeem man*.

The poem is based upon the sixteenth chapter of First

Samuel, King Saul afflicted by the evil spirit. He had made evil king; and now he was in the darkness of his tent, in the very midnight of the soul. Abner brings the young David, "with God's dew on his gracious gold hair," the fresh lilies twined around his harp-strings, that his music might free the spirit of the king. David knelt and prayed and then entered the black tent. The great figure of the king stood motionless and gloomy in the center.

David tuned his harp and played first the songs of nature; the tune that calls the sheep home, the music the quails follow. Then he played the songs of life, the song of the reapers, the funeral dirge for the dead, the marriage hymn, the battle-song, the chorus of the priests. As the music paused, Saul groaned and it seemed as though life were coming back to him.

Then David bent over his harp again and sang. He sang of the beauty of God's world and the joy of living. And finally he began to sing the story of Saul's life, his beauty and strength and brave deeds, the glory of fame and power. And as he came to the end he sounded the name, *"Saul,"* as though it were the shout of a nation. And the blackness rolled away from Saul's soul. Death was past, but life was not yet come. Thus with arms folded across his chest, the king stood. What could the minstrel sing more? How bring to the soul of the awakened king a new life? 'Twas God that gave him the song. He sang the hope of life, of triumph at last. He sang the blessed Gospel that by God's mercy the past may be left forever. Let the old Saul be dead. "In the depth of the vale make his tomb." Let a new Saul arise from the grave of the old.

The young minstrel loves the king; what would he not do to fill this man's life with love and power? And now Browning himself speaks through the words of David, and from the very depths of his soul. Deeper or more sincere utterance never came from the lips of poet. The message is a simple one. Every one can feel its force. Every faculty which I have, God must have in an infinite degree. If I love this man, how God must love him! If I would sacrifice myself to save Saul from his bondage, will God do less?

Would I suffer for him that I love? So would'st Thou,
 so wilt Thou!
So shall crown thee the topmost, ineffablest, uttermost
 crown—
And thy love fill infinitude wholly, nor leave up nor down
One spot for the creature to stand in! It is by no breath,
Turn of eye, wave of hand, that salvation joins issue
 with death!
As thy love is discovered almighty, almighty be proved
Thy power, that exists with and for it, of being beloved!
He who did most, shall bear most; the strongest shall
 stand the most weak.
'Tis the weakness in strength, that I cry for! my flesh
 that I seek
In the Godhead! I seek and I find it. O Saul, it shall be
A Face like my face that receives thee; a Man like to me
Thou shalt love and be loved by, for ever: a Hand like
 this hand
Shall throw open the gates of new life to thee!
 See the Christ stand!

CHAPTER VIII

Matthew Arnold, The Poet of the Questioning Spirit

CHAPTER VIII

MATTHEW ARNOLD, THE POET OF THE QUESTIONING
SPIRIT

Matthew Arnold's closing words concerning Marcus Aurelius, in the volume "Essays in Criticism," might be taken as a truthful characterization of the poet's own life: "We see him wise, just, self-governed, tender, thankful, blameless; yet, with all this, agitated, stretching out his arms to something beyond,—tendentemque manus ripæ ulterioris amore."

When Wordsworth died in 1850, Arnold was twenty-seven and already recognized as a critic. And what he first assayed to do became a lifelong habit. Whatever the form of literature, he was always a critic.

As a poet, Wordsworth no doubt had the greatest influence over his life. Fox Howe, the country house of Thomas Arnold, is in the valley of the Rothay just below Rydal Mount, the last and long home of Wordsworth, and the two families, near neighbors and of kindred tastes, became close frineds. Matthew Arnold from a lad was taught to reverence the poet and the scenes he loved were associated with the person and verse of Wordsworth.

And in April, 1850, on the occasion of the Laureate's death, Arnold wrote the memorial verses in which occurs the fine tribute to his master, and the expression of his critical and questioning melancholy which marked so much of his poetry.

He too upon a wintry clime
Had fallen—on this iron time
Of doubts, disputes, distractions, fears,
He found us when the age had bound
Our souls in its benumbing round:
He spoke, and loosed our heart in tears.
He laid us as we lay at birth
On the cool flowery lap of earth,
Smiles broke from us and we had ease;
The hills were round us, and the breeze
Went o'er the sunlit fields again;
Our foreheads felt the wind and rain.
Our youth return'd; for there was shed
On spirits that had long been dead,
Spirits dried up and closely furl'd,
The freshness of the early world.

Arnold always regarded Wordsworth as his master, yet his reverence and love did not blur his critical vision or blunt the edge of his critical judgment. He was able to separate the gold from the dull ore, and in his selections has given the best of Wordsworth, and in his Introduction a criticism unsurpassed in appreciation and discrimination.

He loved the outdoor world quite as strongly as Wordsworth, but with a different temper. Not so much with the spirit of contemplation as that of pure joy, the sensations of pleasure at form and color. His interest was not so much in studying the impress on his own soul, as in the life itself of plant and animal. His letters are full of descriptions of plants, with their scientific terms, and the physical geography of a new country and its animal and vegetable life he examined with the same interest that he studied man. He loved the good brown earth and his veins tingled with all the

life of the world.   He had full red blood in his veins
and he loved all manly exercises that called him out of
doors.   Such sports as skating, tennis and fly fishing
he kept up with increasing zest to the very end of his
life.

But to understand the man, and especially his attitude
towards the accepted forms of Christian truth, we must
know that he was a critic.   This temper of mind he
carried into all his work.

He was a critic in questions of society and government.   In this respect he was in striking contrast to
Wordsworth.   As a young man, both were Republicans.
Wordsworth was an ardent Republican; his soul was
kindled with hope; he threw himself with an enthusiastic
devotion, with self-abandonment on the side of Republican France.   And though he later turned from politics
to the meditative life of a poet, and was a very staid
and conventional Tory, the fiery impulses of youth left
with him an abiding interest and faith in the essential
worth of every man.   Arnold had the same faith, but
never the same enthusiasm.   His judgment taught him
to read aright the movements of life and to hold to the
rights of man as the true theory of society, but he saw
the weaknesses and the long struggles, and so he was
always more inclined to give advice than to lend a hand.
This attitude is exactly expressed in a poem, "To a
Republican Friend":

> God knows it, I am with you.   If to prize
> Those virtues, prized and practised by too few,
> But prized, but loved, but eminent in you,
> Man's fundamental life; if to despise
>
> The barren optimistic sophistries
> Of comfortable moles, whom what they do

Teaches the limit of the just and true
(And for such doing they require not eyes);

If sadness at the long heart-wasting show
Wherein earth's great ones are disquieted;
If thoughts, not idle, while before me flow

The armies of the homeless and unfed—
If these are yours, if this is what you are,
Then am I yours, and what you feel, I share.

Yet, when I muse on what life is, I seem
Rather to patience prompted, than that proud
Prospect of hope which France proclaims so loud—
  * * * * *
Nor will that day dawn at a human nod,
When, bursting through the network superposed
By selfish occupation—plot and plan,

Lust, avarice, envy—liberated man,
All difference with his fellow-mortal closed,
Shall be left standing face to face with God.

Theoretically he believed in the people and in the extended sphere of the State, but practically he admired the Remnant. He was keen and suggestive in his criticism of national tendencies, but his tastes were with the people of leisure and position. And so he wavered between political principle and social taste, or rather between the two he always stood with a certain cool and self-controlled aloofness. He recognized the cruel wrongs of the Irish people; he pointed them out long before the politicians; but when something practical was attempted, no man could be more critical of the Liberals and of Gladstone's policy. In politics he was critical rather than constructive. He pitied the poor, but he pitied them from above. He was, to use the words of

Goldwin Smith, "a gentleman of a jaunty air, and on good terms with the world," "a Hebrew prophet in white kid gloves."

No doubt Matthew Arnold's best critical work is in literature. Here he is a recognized master. He escaped from provincial bounds more than most English writers. With the English sturdy love of substance and truth, he combined the French love of form. He knew other languages and literatures than English, was as much at home in Homer and Æschylus as Shakspere, in Goethe as Wordsworth. He was a disciple of Sainte-Beuve, the great French critic, and had much of the French temper of mind; over his English seriousness played the light of French grace and wit. He reverenced form with truth, and sometimes allowed his æsthetic taste to be the chief test of worth. He aimed at simplicity but it was sometimes simplesse,—to use the French distinction of Mr. Russell his friend and biographer,—the simulance of simplicity rather than simplicity itself. He had a true love for nature, the truth of the world and of man, but he had to see it through his own eyes and the vision could never be quite freed from the color of the spectacles. As when he calls General Grant a greater man than Abraham Lincoln, and when he speaks of Tennyson as lacking in intellectual qualities. It seemed as though he lacked appreciation for the men of his own age: in the attempt to quicken the English mind and create a pure taste for literature, he exaggerated the worth of foreign literatures, especially the French. Professor Saintsbury shows the error of the critical spirit in commenting on some of Arnold's statements in his "Essays in Criticism": "Here is the astounding statement that 'not very much of current English literature comes into this best that is known and thought in the world. Not very much I fear: certainly less than of the current literature of France and Germany.' And this was 1865, when the Germans had had no great poet but Heine for a generation, nor any great poets but Goethe and Heine for five hundred years. It was 1865 when all the great French writers, themselves of but some thirty years' standing, were dying off, not to be succeeded! Eighteen-sixty-five, when for seventy years England had not lacked, and for nearly thirty more was not to lack, poets and prose writers of the first order by the dozen and almost by the score."

Nevertheless Arnold was a keen and kind critic. He had a genuine appreciation of the great names of our language and he knew them. He had a horror of unreality. He impaled the "desperate endeavors to render a platitude endurable by making it pompous." He held up a pure standard to a generation of writers. Better Introduction to literature cannot be found than such essays as those on Wordsworth and Milton. He is worthy of Mr. Russell's estimate: "Whatever may be thought of the substance of his writings, it surely must be admitted that he was a great master of style. And his style was altogether his own. In the last year of his life, he said to the present writer, 'People think I can teach them style. What stuff it all is! Have something to say, and say it as clearly as you can. That is the only secret of style.'"

The critical temper which we have seen in politics and literature, Matthew Arnold brought into questions of religion. He took upon himself the serious task of being the mentor of his countrymen. And his criticisms of religion such as "Literature and Dogma" are probably his best known writings and have had the greatest influence on our time. He certainly desired the truth in religion. But he looked at the Bible and the doctrines of Protestantism as a literary man and a critic; and he emphasized the human elements and the literary qualities and ignored or denied the supernatural; and his critical temper led him to accept the latest views of authorship and message without the sufficient knowledge to form a critical estimate. His admiration for foreign literatures put him easily under the influence of Renan and Strauss. He was certainly influenced too much by the dilettante attitude of Renan.

There is no keener criticism of Matthew Arnold's position in religion than that by Mr. Carnegie Simpson in his "The Fact of Christ." He speaks of the most serious and influential modern criticism of Christianity as professedly reconstructive. "It desires not the ruin of Christianity but its rescue. It would give us the true and simple and pure Christian religion in place of the beclouded and corrupt tradition of the centuries. . . . I hope it may be said without offense that to one with any grave historical sense there is something about this that savors a little of what might be described as intellectual *nouvelle richesse*. To propose to take down the structure of a Christianity that has stood for centuries, and to rebuild it largely anew, to allege that the main idea of the thing has been radically misconstrued, and needs to be started afresh, to say that the lines laid down and followed by St. John and St. Paul, by Athanasius, Augustine, Luther, are largely misleading and a new direction at this hour of the day must be taken,—one cannot help feeling that all this, like the philosophy of the man who has struck oil, lacks historic background. Under what a melancholy mistake have these nineteen centuries been laboring!

On what a false scent those apostles put us! what a pity that St. John, 'who was so much more metaphysical than his Master,' was ever allowed to write about Him, or that St. Paul, whom the older rationalism held to be the real creator of Christianity, appeared just at the critical, formative moment he did in Christian history! And how thankful we should be that now, at last, such a clever and still ingenuous man as the author of Literature and Dogma has come to put us right. . . . These reconstructions have many aspects of value, for the Church is constantly in danger of being a slave to its past and of thinking that a quotation from a Father or a confession is the final word of truth. But it does not do to put a fool's cap on the history of the Christian religion."

Underneath the "easy, sinuous, unpolemical" style of the essays one can feel the high purpose of Mr. Arnold; and he has taught us to regard the Bible with more genuine human interest. "To understand that the language of the Bible is fluid, passing and literary, not rigid, fixed and scientific, is the first step towards the right understanding of the Bible. But to take this very step, some experience of how men have thought and expressed themselves, and some flexibility of spirit, are necessary; and this is culture." He has put some of his criticism in unforgettable phrase: "When we are asked, What is the object of religion?—let us reply, *Conduct.* And when we are asked further, What is conduct?—Let us answer, Three-fourths of life." "The true meaning of religion is not simply morality, but *morality touched by emotion.*" "They had dwelt upon the thought of conduct and right and wrong, till the *not ourselves* which is in us and all around us, became to them adorable eminently and altogether as a *power which makes for righteousness,* which makes for it unchangeably and eternally, and is therefore called the eternal." His affirmations were often strongly religious, but his negations were often influenced by the distaste for the dogmatism and what he called the Philistinism of the Dissenters. He did not have Browning's faith to see the spiritual realities beneath creed and form and even ignorant enthusiasm.

> Better have knelt at the poorest stream
> That trickles in pain from the straitest rift!
> For the less or the more is all God's gift.

But despite his negative criticism and his unwillingness to attribute personality to God, Matthew Arnold was a good man, reverencing the character of Christ, trying to conform his life to his law. "His theology, once the subject of such animated criticism, seems now a matter of little moment; for indeed his nature was essentially religious. He was loyal to truth as he knew it, loved the light and sought it earnestly, and by his daily and hourly practice gave sweet and winning illustration of his own doctrine that conduct is three-fourths of human life." (Russell, p. 264.)

Matthew Arnold has never been a popular poet. He has been read by only a few, and even they differ as to his future. Within certain limits he was a true poet and he had a strong faith in the future of his poetry. He says in a letter to his mother in 1869: "My poems represent on the whole the main movement of mind of the last quarter of a century, and they will thus probably have their day as people become more conscious to themselves of what that movement of mind is, and interested in the literary productions which re-

flect it. It might be fairly urged that I have less poetical sentiment than Tennyson and less intellectual vigor
and abundance than Browning; yet because I have perhaps more of a fusion of the two than either of them,
and have more regularly applied that fusion to the
main line of modern development, I am likely enough
to have my turn, as they have had theirs." Such a
letter as this, and his well-known definition of poetry
as "a criticism of life," tell us why he did not write
much poetry and why he did not speak to the heart
of man. He was too much a critic to be a poet in an
ample sense. He was never disturbed, never profoundly
moved. He could never give himself unreservedly to
any cause. He was not simple and sensuous and passionate. But more than this he was not hopeful and
joyful. He had a half melancholy contemplation of
life. And poetry that is a message of life is born of
a great hope and faith.

His first book of poetry, 1849, when he was twenty-
six, is a most remarkable first book. But he wrote little poetry and with much difficulty. Most of it was
written before he was thirty-five. And though he re-
peatedly vows to turn to what he always called his true
vocation, he wrote almost nothing of value the last
thirty years of his life. His laborious duties of school
inspector no doubt in part account for this lack of pro-
duction, but his critical, not creative, temper, far more.
Poetry was not a passion.

But Arnold was sensitive to his age, and the poetry
of his youth, responsive to the intellectual voices of his
time, was full of the questioning spirit. The philosophy
born of new science refused to state its doctrine of
God and man in the old forms. The new spirit of criticism was calling nothing sacred, nothing profane, mak-

ing of the most sacred facts and truths an experiment. And without losing his moral earnestness, his devotion to duty, Arnold reflected the intellectual uncertainty of men. In his poetry he combines a melancholy agnosticism as to the truths of revealed religion, with an asceticism, seen in the almost Doric plainness of his verse, and his stern holding to the moral truths of Christianity, whose spiritual truths were so uncertain to his mind. Arnold was under the scientific thought and philosophic thought of the day: that man is an inseparable part of the creation; the new idealism, that man is an expression of the all-spirit, and at t'mes the thought somewhat denies the conception of personality.

> Spirit, who fillest all!
> Spirit, who utterest in each
> New-coming son of mankind
> Such of thy thoughts as thou wilt!
> O thou, one of whose moods,
> Bitter and strange, was the life
> Of Heine,—his strange, alas,
> His bitter life!—may a life
> Other and milder be mine!
> May'st thou a mood more serene,
> Happier, have utter'd in mine!
> May'st thou the rapture of peace
> Deep have embreathed at its core;
> Made it a ray of thy thought,
> Made it a beat of thy joy!

One of his earliest poems ("To Fausta") expresses his questioning view of life.

> Joy comes and goes, hope ebbs and flows
> Like the wave!

Change doth unknit the tranquil strength of men.
　　Love lends life a little grace,
　　A few sad smiles; and then,
　　Both are laid in one cold place,
　　　　In the grave.

Dreams dawn and fly, friends smile and die
　　Like spring flowers:
Our vaunted life is one long funeral.
　　Men dig graves with bitter tears
　　For their dead hopes; and all,
　　Mazed with doubts and sick with fears,
　　　　Count the hours.

We count the hours! These dreams of ours,
　　False and hollow,
Do we go hence and find they are not dead?
　　Joys we dimly apprehend,
　　Faces that smiled and fled,
　　Hopes born here, and born to end,
　　　　Shall we follow?

It is not a jaunty, light-hearted spirit of questioning.
There is a sad sincerity about it. Arnold feels with
pain the loss of the simple faith of childhood.

　　　From the ingrain'd fashion
　　　Of this earthly nature
　　　That mars thy creature;
　　　From grief that is but passion,
　　　From mirth that is but feigning,
　　　From tears that bring no healing,
　　　From wild and weak complaining,
　　　　Thine old strength revealing,
　　　　　Save, oh! save.
　　　From doubt, where all is double;
　　　Where wise men are not strong,

Where comfort turns to trouble,
Where just men suffer wrong;
Where sorrow treads on joy,
Where sweet things soonest cloy,
Where faiths are built on dust,
Where love is half mistrust,
Hungry, and barren, and sharp as the sea—
Oh! set us free.
O let the false dream fly,
Where our sick souls do lie
Tossing continually!

("Stagirius")

He feels the hopeless tangle of the age, and yet he is sure of one thing, that the only path of light is the way of sacrifice. The lines "In Memory of the Author of Obermann" tell us this.

He who hath watch'd, not shared, the strife,
Knows how the day hath gone.
He only lives with the world's life,
Who hath renounced his own.

No man has pictured more vividly and genuinely the pain of a dying faith. He had not lacked teachers who had shown him the high, white stars of truth, but now faith is

But a dead time's exploded dream.

In the high Alps, in the silence of the Grande Chartreuse, among a people who believe, he cannot escape the restlessness of his own heart:

Wandering between two worlds, one dead,
The other powerless to be born,
With nowhere yet to rest my head,
Like these, on earth, I wait forlorn.

But nowhere is the pathos of a faithless world, together
with the clinging to love and duty as the best of life so
wonderfully expressed as in the lines on "Dover
Beach." No verses are charged with truer feeling, and
his life speaks so strongly as to attain the most perfect
lyric form. English poetry has rarely reached such
realism, the picture of the outer world of nature, and
the inner world of a man's heart.

The sea is calm to-night.
The tide is full, the moon lies fair
Upon the straits;—on the French coast the light
Gleams and is gone; the cliffs of England stand,
Glimmering and vast, out in the tranquil bay.
Come to the window, sweet is the night-air!
Only, from the long line of spray
Where the sea meets the moon-blanch'd land,
Listen! you hear the grating roar
Of pebbles which the waves draw back, and fling,
At their return, up the high strand.
Begin, and cease, and then again begin,
With tremulous cadence slow, and bring
The eternal note of sadness in.

Sophocles long ago
Heard it on the Ægean, and it brought
Into his mind the turbid ebb and flow
Of human misery; we
Find also in the sound a thought,
Hearing it by this distant northern sea.

The Sea of Faith
Was once, too, at the full, and round earth's shore
Lay like the folds of a bright girdle furl'd!
But now I only hear
Its melancholy, long, withdrawing roar,
Retreating, to the breath
Of the night-wind, down the vast edges drear
And naked shingles of the world.

Ah, love, let us be true
To one another! for the world, which seems
To lie before us like a land of dreams,
So various, so beautiful, so new,
Hath really neither joy, nor love, nor light,
Nor certitude, nor peace, nor help for pain;
And we are here as on a darkling plain
Swept with confused alarms of struggle and flight,
Where ignorant armies clash by night.

Arnold never used criticism for the joy of seeing the structure of faith tumble. If he seemed largely destructive, it was that the temporary might be removed, and religion rest upon eternal foundations. He held that the old forms of faith had been blown away by the age-spirit, and he hoped to see a truer and stronger faith rise in its stead. In the poem "Obermann once more": the Old World before Christianity was a world dead in its sin:

On that hard Pagan world disgust
And secret loathing fell.
Deep weariness and sated lust
Made human life a hell.

Christianity began to make a new world out of the ruins of the old:

So well she mused, a morning broke
Across her spirit grey;
A conquering, new-born joy awoke,
And fill'd her life with day.

Arnold felt the glory of the change.   He almost felt
himself born too late.

Oh, had I lived in that great day,
How had its glory new
Fill'd earth and heaven, and caught away
My ravished spirit too!

*   *   *   *   *

While we believed, on earth he went,
And open stood his grave.
Men call'd from chamber, church, and tent;
And Christ was by to save.

But that was a story of the past.   Men could not have
that faith in the light of to-day.

Now he is dead!   Far hence he lies
In the lorn Syrian town;
And on his grave, with shining eyes,
The Syrian stars look down.

But the needs of men are the same, the religious nature
and craving are universal.   There must be a Power, to
make all things new.

The millions suffer still, and grieve.
And what can helpers heal
With old-world cures men half believe
For woes they wholly feel?

And yet men have such need of joy!
But joy whose grounds are true;
And joy that should all hearts employ
As when the past was new.

And Arnold puts his hope into the mouth of Obermann,
who fled to the wilderness to find rest from the weariness of the age-spirit that Arnold felt, that round his
manhood hung the "weeds of our sad time"—

Despair not thou as I despair'd,
Nor be cold gloom thy prison!
Forward the gracious hours have fared,
And see! the sun is risen!

He breaks the winter of the past;
A green, new earth appears.
Millions, whose life in ice lay fast,
Have thoughts, and smiles, and tears.

What though there still need effort, strife?
Though much be still unwon?
Yet warm it mounts, the hour of life!
Death's frozen hour is done!

That's the hope of Arnold, but the light is never very
clear nor the substance of his faith very firm. He was
always a man wandering between two worlds, "the one
dead, the other powerless to be born." Compare
Arnold's sentimental sadness in "Growing Old"—

To spend long days
And not once feel that we were ever young,—

with Browning's splendid optimism born of his sturdy
faith:

Grow old along with me!
The best is yet to be,
The last of life, for which the first was made:
Our times are in His hand
Who saith "A whole I planned,
Youth shows but half; trust God: see all,
      nor be afraid!"

Or compare Arnold's dim hope through mournful lines of his "Self-Deception" with the clear shining of Wordsworth's faith in his "Immortality."

There is no abiding and uplifting joy in Arnold and there could not be with his questioning spirit, but he was a Christian Stoic (if two such seemingly contradictory words may be put together), and the great message of his life was duty, and he was an unflinching example of it. And under duty he would include truth and work and love.

He felt the glory of loving service. He had moments when his heart fully responded to the life of faith. Witness his "East London":

'Twas August, and the fierce sun overhead
Smote on the squalid streets of Bethnal Green,
And the pale weaver, through his windows seen
In Spitalfields, look'd thrice dispirited.

I met a preacher there I knew, and said:
"Ill and o'erwork'd, how fare you in this scene?"
"Bravely!" said he; "for I of late have been
Much cheered with thoughts of Christ, *the living bread.*"

O human soul! as long as thou canst so
Set up a mark of everlasting light,
Above the howling senses' ebb and flow,

To cheer thee, and to right thee if thou roam—
Not with lost toil thou labourest through the night!
Thou mak'st the heaven thou hop'st indeed thy home.

He felt the greatness of his father's faith and life,
and "Rugby Chapel" is the tribute of a reverent and
loyal son. He himself was only a storm-beaten figure
who had hardly fought himself through to the lonely
inn 'mid the rocks.

> Friends, companions, and train,
> The avalanche swept from our side.

But the son feels that his father, the great school-
master of Rugby is a more heroic figure.

> But thou would'st not *alone*
> Be saved, my father! *alone*
> Conquer and come to thy goal,
> Leaving the rest in the wild.
> We were weary, and we
> Fearful, and we in our march
> Fain to drop down and to die.
> Still thou turnedst, and still
> Gavest the weary thy hand.
>
> If, in the paths of the world,
> Stones might have wounded thy feet,
> Toil or dejection have tried
> Thy spirit, of that we saw
> Nothing—to us thou wast still
> Cheerful, and helpful, and firm!
> Therefore to thee it was given
> Many to save with thyself;
> And, at the end of thy day,
> O faithful shepherd! to come,
> Bringing thy sheep in thy hand.

Matthew Arnold lived too much in the mists and storms of the questioning spirit to be the shepherd of others, but it is pleasant to think of him as gaining the shelter of the fold at last. His conduct was governed by deeply religious motives, he did not neglect the offices of religion because his critical reason could not always accept as truth the creed of the Church, and he claimed as his inheritance the great traditions of fellowship and of worship.

The last Sunday of his life he was staying with a friend in Liverpool and went with his host to the morning service at the Sefton Park Presbyterian Church, of which Dr. John Watson was then pastor. He stayed to the communion service at which Watts' hymn was sung,

When I survey the wondrous Cross.

He was deeply impressed with the combined simplicity and reverence of the Scotch communion and said to his friend on the way home that he thought Watts' hymn the noblest hymn in the English language. And as he went up the stairs to his room one of the servants in the hall heard him quietly repeating to himself,

When I survey the wondrous Cross
On which the Prince of Glory died,
My richest gain I count but loss,
And pour contempt on all my pride.

CHAPTER IX

Poets of Doubt and Denial

CHAPTER IX

POETS OF DOUBT AND DENIAL

In Browning's philosophy, his attempt to reconcile human sin and misery with a goal of infinite love, he says that evil may be the foil of good, as light needs shade. It is certain that we shall feel the beauty and glory of the spring as they cannot understand who live in sunny climes. The winter of our discontent shall give place to glorious summer.

English poetry has its moods, and we must go through all of them to understand its message. In the last chapter we dwelt in the twilight shade of Arnold's questioning spirit. Now we must enter the deepening shadows of doubt and denial, until we are in the black midnight of the soul. We shall console ourselves with the thought that morning cometh.

I

Arthur Hugh Clough was associated all his too brief life with Matthew Arnold. They were schoolboys together at Rugby; they went to the same university; they had many noble friendships in common; they loved the same scenes and storied places; they had many similar ideals, and they finally engaged in the same life-work. They were both sensitive and true and deeply religious. Reverencing truth and their own souls, they met the critical influences hostile to old faiths without flinching, yet often sore perplexed. They were like ships in the teeth of wind and wave, stoutly weathering the gale, but with strippéd decks and rent cordage and driven far from their course.

Matthew Arnold has connected the life of Clough with the story of the scholar-gypsy, the tradition of the university man, weary of the world of thought, reacing from the hopeless effort to penetrate the problem of life, giving it all up and following the care-free life of a gypsy. That's only one phase of Clough, but it does interpret the revulsion of mind from too much thinking. "Thyrsis," the beautiful elegy that Arnold wrote on the death of Clough, continues the figure blended with the early and sweet note of nature.

> What though the music of thy rustic flute
> Kept not for long its happy, country tone;
> Lost it too soon, and learnt a stormy note
> Of men contention-tost, of men who groan,
> Which task'd thy pipe too sore, and tired thy throat—
>   It failed, and thou wast mute!
> Yet hadst thou alway visions of our light,
> And long with men of care thou couldst not stay,
> And soon thy foot resumed its wandering way,
> Left human haunt, and on alone till night.

Clough was a favorite pupil of Thomas Arnold and easily won all the honors that Rugby could give. He went up to Oxford with the promise of a most brilliant career, but failed to win the coveted place at Balliol, though afterward elected a fellow of Oriel. It was the restless heart, the uncertainty at the foundations of life, that withheld for him the rightful completion of his powers, that stayed his career short of its highest and fullest expression. Life was too intense. He thought too much without the natural relief and balance of action. He felt the pressure of moral responsibility too early. He made an impossible demand upon his own nature and upon Christian truth. His business was to find truth, and until he could have the certainty of truth under the new conditions, he could have no assured faith. He regarded life too intently as a problem to be thought out, instead of a simple duty to be acted out.

And when Clough was at Oxford, the influence of John Henry Newman was at its height. It was intensely religious and a reaction from progressive thought in the Church and in the State. It was a religious and political Toryism. Newman and the Oxford Movement stood for authority in creed and Church. It would admit of no religion apart from dogmatic belief. And here was the very difficulty of men like Arnold and Clough. To their minds scientific and historical criticism had affected the facts on which the creeds were built. The truth of religion must be found not in the creeds of the Church but in the experience of the soul. Clough's mind reacted from all authority. He did not believe that any group of minds could ever fix the form of truth. Matthew Arnold found more relief in action, in literature and society and public life. The uncertainty of faith was not such a malady of soul. But Clough's more contemplative life, and its narrower interest, made the inner world of thought supreme, and in that inner world the vital question was one of faith. He always had the attitude of the learner. "Reverent waiting for light not yet given, respect for the truth so absolute that nothing doubtful can be accepted as truth because it is pleasant to the soul" made the waiting painful in the uncertain theories and confused thinking of his day. "He never denied the reality of much that he himself could not use as spiritual nutriment. He believed that God spoke differently to different ages and different minds. Not therefore could he lay aside his own duty of seeking and waiting."

As a fellow and tutor of Oriel College, Oxford, Clough had to subscribe to the Thirty-nine Articles of the Church of England. The thought of the slightest intellectual insincerity did not add to his peace of mind. And the life in Oxford, agreeable as much of it was to his intellectual and social tastes, he felt as a sort of repression. The meeting with Mr. Ralph Waldo Emerson in 1847, whose writings found a kindred spirit, and the forming of an intimate friendship with this sturdiest of non-conformists, was a strong influence on Clough towards freedom and independence. And he resigned his Oxford living and became principal of University Hall, London, largely under control of Unitarians. But he did not find here the freedom which his questioning spirit craved. With Clough, it was not so much the questioning of old forms, as the quest of truth. And he found the dogmatism of denial quite as intolerant and irksome as the dogmatism of assertion. He gave up his London work and came to America to try a new life. He found a home in Cambridge and busied himself with pupils and in writing for reviews. His short stay in this country was not notable for the work he did, but for the friends he made, and the impress he made upon them of his pure and gifted nature. Mr. Lowell, in his tribute to Agassiz, has caught the very features of Clough, the picture of the man's soul, as he appeared to that noble group of poets and thinkers and friends.

> And he our passing guest,
> Shy nature, too, and stung with life's unrest,
> Whom we too briefly had but could not hold,
>
>   *   *   *
>
> Boy face, but grave with answerless desires,
> Poet in all that poets have of best,
> But foiled with riddles dark and cloudy aims.

Mr. Clough was called back to England by the offer of a place in the Education Office, and he spent his remaining years, like Matthew Arnold, in the difficult and practical work of building up a people's education for England. He married and had a happy home; children grew up around him, and though the short years were in much weakness and a constant fight for life, the restless heart knew what joy meant and the questioning spirit found some truth precious. He was not now breaking his heart over endless and fruitless speculation, but was able to rest somewhat in the deep spiritual facts of life. Before this the mind had been too free to deal with the spiritual problems of the world. Now practical duties calmed the spirit and led him into practical faith, if not into unquestioned belief.

I have rehearsed these simple facts of Clough's life, for without them the message of his poetry cannot be understood. No poet is more personal in his verse. And for this reason he has never been read by many, but by a few he has been greatly loved in proportion as they have found their own lives interpreted by his self-revelations.

Clough is buried close by Wordsworth in the little Churchyard at Grasmere, and in his love of nature he was a pupil of Wordsworth. He had the same love of lonely places; nature spoke to his heart, and he brooded over the impress that nature made upon him. But his real world was within. He felt the pathos of the world's struggle and poverty and pain, and he had the vision of a new world fairer and happier. He felt the call of the wider brotherhood. But the chief problem of life was in his own heart. And his chief interest for the student of life and literature is in that he mirrors so fully the wonder and query and quest of a sensitive and sincere mind at the new facts and philosophies of life that refuse to be stated in the old terms of faith.

All testify to the beauty of his soul and the purity of his character. A more naturally devout man never lived. Religion was his life. Yet religion had rested upon certain teachings of the Bible and the Church. If these teachings were discredited or changed what could give the soul the sense of God and the divine authority for conduct? He would believe and yet he would only believe on sufficient grounds. He would not make his judgment blind. He would not force the assent of his soul. And he could not answer the call of men until he had settled the supreme question of faith. And so through all his early manhood Clough questioned and balanced and wavered. The creative power of the poet missed the impulse and joy of clear vision. He was less of a poet because of this endless quest of the intellect. His sympathy for human need missed the motive of positive faith. He served less because he could not take one step until the whole way was made plain. He was indeed a "perturbed spirit," the Hamlet among poets. He often felt

> The time is out of joint; O cursed spite!
> That ever I was born to set it right.

His early poems constantly reflect his restless spirit.

> How often sit I, poring o'er
> My strange distorted youth,
> Seeking in vain, in all my store,
> One feeling based on truth;
> Amid the maze of petty life
> A clue whereby to move,
> A spot whereon in toil and strife
> To dare to rest and love.
> So constant as my heart would be,
> So fickle as it must,
> 'Twere well for others as for me
> 'Twere dry as summer dust.
> Excitements come, and act and speech
> Flow freely forth;—but no,
> Nor they, nor aught beside can reach
> The buried world below.

Though knowledge is uncertain, though the mind struggles in vain for the certitude of faith, life moves on, it is a part of the stream ever "descending to the sea."

> O end to which our currents tend,
>   Inevitable sea,
> To which we flow, what do we know,
>   What shall we guess of thee?
>
> A roar we hear upon thy shore,
>   As we our course fulfil;
> Scarce we divine a sun will shine
>   And be above us still.
>   ("The Stream of Life")

This earthly life must be followed. There may be little joyful light upon it, but duty is ours, the duty of relationships and work. And though we may not have the beckoning of a clear-shining goal, we must follow on in the trust that we shall arrive.

> Whate'er you dream with doubt possessed,
> Keep, keep it snug within your breast,
> And lay you down and take your rest;
> Forget in sleep the doubt and pain,
> And when you wake, to work again.
> The wind it blows, the vessel goes,
> And where and wither, no one knows.
>
> 'T will all be well: no need of care;
> Though how it will, and when and where,
> We can not see, and can't declare.
> In spite of dreams, in spite of thought,
> 'Tis not in vain, and not for naught,
> The wind it blows, the ship it goes,
> Though where and whither, no one knows.
>
> ("All's Well")

The questioning spirit that gives a tone of melancholy to all the earlier work of Clough, sometimes gathers thick clouds and shuts down upon the path and hides all hope. That is true of "Easter Day," written in Naples in 1849.

> Ashes to ashes, dust to dust;
> As of the unjust, also of the just—
>   Yea, of that Just One, too!
> This is the one sad Gospel that is true—
>   Christ is not risen!

*   *   *

Eat, drink and die, for we are souls bereaved:
Of all the creatures under heaven's wide cope
We are most hopeless, who had once most hope,
And most beliefless, that had most believed.
    Ashes to ashes, dust to dust;
As of the unjust, also of the just—
    Yea, of that Just One, too!
It is the one sad Gospel that is true—
    Christ is not risen!

      *   *   *   *   *

Here, on our Easter Day
We rise, we come, and lo; we find Him not,
Gardner nor other, on the sacred spot:
Where they have laid Him there is none to say:
No sound, nor in, nor out—no word
Of where to seek the dead or meet the living Lord.
There is no glistering of an angel's wings,
There is no voice of heavenly clear behest:
Let us go hence, and think upon these things
    In silence, which is best.
    Is He not risen? No—
    But lies and moulders low?
    Christ is not risen?

You notice that the poem does not end with the negative of denial, but with the interrogative of uncertainty,
through which the heart will speak its hope. And when,
as I have said, Clough had regular work that engaged
his best powers and was felt to be of large service to
his fellows; above all when he had a happy home and
interests that won his heart, the intellectual problems
of religion were no longer considered apart from the
life of love and obedience. He did not then throw
himself against the limitations of knowledge and recoil
bruised and bleeding, and he found much of the rest

of Him who is meek and lowly of heart, and who has taught that love is the school of the highest knowledge.

The second "Easter Day" has a different spirit.

> So in the sinful streets, abstracted and alone,
> I with my secret self held communing of mine own.
> So in the southern city spake the tongue
> Of one that somewhat overwildly sung,
> But in a later hour I sat and heard
> Another voice that spake—and this graver word.
> Weep not, it bade, whatever hath been said,
> Though He be dead, He is not dead.
>> In the true creed
>> He is yet risen indeed;
>> Christ is yet risen.

The spirit of hope could never die out, the precious heritage of his white soul, the comrade of his life of love. Thomas Arnold speaks of the beautiful poem beginning

> Say not the struggle naught availeth,

that it was written during his last illness in Italy, in his vain search for health. In his collected poems it is the last, but dated 1849. And Mr. Stopford Brooke speaks of it as the product of his earlier days, and of the hopeful spirit that could not perish. It is the most precious verse of Clough, and prophesies of what he might have done had he lived with a freer spirit.

> Say not the struggle naught availeth,
> The labor and the wounds are vain,
> The enemy faints not, nor faileth,
> And as things have been they remain.

If hopes were dupes, fears may be liars;
It may be, in yon smoke concealed,
Your comrades chase e'en now the fliers,
And, but for you, possess the field.

For while the tired waves, vainly breaking,
Seem here no painful inch to gain,
Far back, through creeks and inlets making,
Comes silent, flooding in, the main.

And not by Eastern windows only,
When daylight comes, comes in the light,
In front, the sun climbs slow, how slowly,
But westward, look, the land is bright.

"What the image suggested became true as the years
of the century went on. It is even truer now. We
have a closer, more faithful grasp on truth than Clough
could have; we have a diviner and a clearer hope. And
what the last verse says was realized also, one is glad
to think, in his own life." (S. Brooke, p. 51.)

II

WILLIAM ERNEST HENLEY (1849-1903)

Mr. Henley has made his impress by the spirit of
his poetry rather than the richness of its thought or
the perfection of its form. He has left but one thin
volume—though I think many stray pieces have not
been collected—but that volume has gone through many
editions because it finds the heart that loves the world
and feels its beauty, that loves life and wishes to play
the man, yet feels the pathos of its mystery and incom-
pleteness and tragedy. It is the purpose to find the
utmost beauty and joy out of the brief and painful life

of man, to know human love and duty in the face of the unknowable and immeasurable forces of the world, to preserve the self inviolate, to have the unconquerable will in the clutch of circumstance, that has made Henley's poems the personal message to so many men of our time.

Clough was essentially a religious poet. As I have said, a soul more naturally devout never lived. And his songs were always about himself, about the problems of God and duty as they affected his own life. It was the inner problem on which he was ever thinking. And this makes his peculiar charm as likewise his weakness and limitation. But God and the spiritual world were mysterious *facts* to him, not a great perhaps. How he should understand these facts in the light of modern knowledge was the question. He never lost hope that the truth could be found, but could it be through the historic forms in which he had been trained? Clough, like Arnold, was a poet of the questioning spirit.

But Henley went a step farther. There is no trace in his poems of the struggle after religious truth. Neither is there any blank and defiant denial. God and the immortal life are beyond his knowledge. There is no evidence that the heavens have been opened. On every side is the wall of the sensible and material through which man cannot go in his search for truth. But this life we have, short and troubled, a vale between two eternities. It is yet a spiritual life; the spirit of man is the chief force in it. How shall we regard it? And what shall we make of it? This is the message of Henley. He is the poet of the *agnostic spirit*.

Henley devoted himself to literature as poet and critic. His early work was associated with Robert

Louis Stevenson in the writing of plays. But this rather uncertain living led him to journalism as a vocation. He became successively the editor of a magazine of art, the *National Observer,* and the *New Review.* He compiled the "Lyra Heroica," an anthology of English verse for boys, and also wrote a dictionary of slang.

His poems are unequal, passing from pure music, the love and joy of life, such as—

> It was a bowl of roses:
> There in the light they lay,
> Languishing, glorying, glowing
> Their life away.
> And the soul of them rose like a presence,
> Into me crept and grew,
> And filled me with something, someone,
> O, was it you?—

to the stirring, rugged verse, calls to duty and heroism, as in the patriotic lyric to R. F. B., closing with the stanzas:

Who says that we shall pass, or the fame of us fade and
    die,
While the living stars fulfil their round in the living sky?
For the sire lives in his sons, and they pay their father's
    debt,
And the Lion has left a whelp wherever his claw was set;
And the Lion in his whelps, his whelps that none shall
    brave,
Is but less strong than Time and the great, all-whelming
    grave.

Or in the more personal lyric, closing with the lines:

Life—give me life until the end,
That at the very top of being,
The battle spirit shouting in my blood,
Out of the reddest hell of the fight
I may be snatched and flung
Into the everlasting lull,
The immortal, incommunicable dream.

And then there is sometimes the rough, unmusical realism that comes from "nervous impressionism." The
series of poems, "In a Hospital," is full of these vivid
touches. The twenty-fifth is "Apparition," perhaps the
most interesting, because it is supposed to apply to
R. L. Stevenson.

Thin-legged, thin-chested, slight unspeakably,
Neat-footed and weak-fingered: in his face—
Lean, large-boned, curved of beak, and touched with race,
Bold-lipped, rich-tinted, mutable as the sea,
The brown eyes radiant with vivacity—
There shines a brilliant and romantic grace,
A spirit intense and rare, with trace on trace
Of passion and impudence and energy.
Valiant in velvet, light in ragged luck,
Most vain, most generous, sternly critical,
Buffoon and poet, lover and sensualist:
A deal of Ariel, just a streak of Puck,
Much Antony, of Hamlet most of all,
And something of the Shorter-Catechist.

This description of Stevenson suggests Henley's
fondness for blunt truth. He published in the *Pall
Mall Gazette* a criticism of Balfour's "Life of Stevenson." "I take a view of Stevenson which declines to
be concerned with this seraph in chocolate, this barley-
sugar effigy of a real man." Then he gave a catalog

of his failings, which he felt was a vindication of his
friend.   He was equally frank concerning Burns, calling him an inspired poet, but also a lewd peasant, and
a cad.

In a narrow sphere Henley was a poet of vivid impression and strong, impulsive expression.   But he was
without the patience and balance to make his work the
highest art.   This lack of patience and thoroughness
that hinder the balanced critic and the growth of the
poet is no doubt connected with the lack of the larger
vision that belonged to faith.   He did not walk humbly
before a world he could not understand.   He refused
to believe what he could not see.   He mistook his personal expressions for the limit of the truth.

There is no hope in Henley, and the joy is chiefly the
memory of the joy that has been, a kind of Stoic joy,
a faint blush of light at the close of a dark and stormy
day.   There is sweetness and beauty, but it is clothed
in sackcloth.

Life is bitter.   All the faces of the years,
Young and old, are gray with travail and with tears.
Must we only wake to toil, to tire, to weep?
In the sun, among the leaves, upon the flowers,
Slumber stills to dreamy death the heavy hours,—
    Let me sleep.

Riches won but mock the old, unable years;
Fame's a pearl that hides beneath a sea of tears;
Love must wither, or must live alone and weep.
In the sunshine, through the leaves, across the flowers,
While we slumber, death approaches through the hours—
    Let me sleep.

Henley knew what wedded love meant and he must
have known a true home, and the heaven-sent life of a

little child, and there is hardly anything more pathetic than the Epilogue to the volume, where the heart-breaking loss of a child is treated with the faintest shadow of hope.

> These, to you now, O, more than ever now—
> Now that the ancient enemy
> Has passed, and we, we two that are one, have seen
> A piece of perfect life
> Turn to so ravishing a shape of death.
> The Arch-Discomforter might well have smiled
> In pity and pride,
> Even as he bore his lovely and innocent spoil
> From those home-kingdoms he left desolate!
> Poor windlestraws
> On the great, sullen, roaring pool of Time
> And Chance and Change, I knew!
> But they are yours, as I am, till we attain
> That end for which we make, we two that are one:
> A little, exquisite ghost
> Between us, smiling with the serenest eyes
> Seen in this world, and calling, calling still
> In that clear voice whose infinite subtleties
> Of sweetness, thrilling back across the grave,
> Break this poor heart to hear:—
>   "Come, Dadsie, come!
> Mama, how long,—how long!"

Henley was a strong, tender, brave man, if somewhat too self-confident and defiant, and the most characteristic note and the best note is the call to life and duty.

> Some starlit garden gray with dew,
> Some chamber flushed with wine and fire,
> What matters where, so I and you
>   Are worthy our desire?

Behind, a past that scolds and jeers
For ungirt loins and lamps unlit;
In front, the unmanageable years,
    The trap upon the Pit;

Think on the shame of dreams for deeds,
The scandal of unnatural strife,
The slur upon immortal needs,
    The treason done to life:

Arise! no more a living lie,
And with me quicken and control
Some memory that shall magnify
    The universal soul.

Life itself is great and worthy, and his motto would be, "To thyself be true." And the individual is bound with others and his highest motive is to "magnify the universal soul." This is the thought in the noble tribute to his mother:

Dearest, live on
In such an immortality
As we thy sons,
Born of thy body and nursed
At those wild, faithful breasts,
Can give—of generous thoughts,
And honorable words, and deeds
That make men half in love with fate!
Live on, O brave and true,
In us thy children, in ours whose life is thine—
Our best and theirs! What is that best but thee—
Thee, and thy gift to us, to pass
Like light along the infinite of space
To the immitigable end?

In all his poetry is the assertion of the individual. Where in poetry is there a more triumphant and defiant tone of individualism than in Henley's tribute to Mr. Hamilton Bruce!

Out of the night that covers me,
Black as the pit from pole to pole,
I thank whatever Gods may be
For my unconquerable soul.

In the fell clutch of circumstance
I have not winced nor cried aloud,
Under the bludgeonings of chance
My head is bloody, but unbowed.

Beyond this place of wrath and tears
Looms but the horror of the shade,
And yet the menace of the years
Finds, and shall find, me unafraid.

It matters not how strait the gate,
How charged with punishments the scroll;
I am the master of my fate:
I am the captain of my soul.

The triumphant or gloomy individualism, the spirit of a Henley or of Davidson and Thomson, is not the whole truth of life. It is a partial because self-centered view. No man can be a man alone. Life is also a matter of relationships. We find that fullest realization of self as we enter into the larger life of the race. And that life has a direction and a force not ourselves into which we are to enter with humility and desire. Over against the dauntless egoism of Henley, or the black pessimism of Davidson or Thomson, I would put the reverent altruism of John Oxenham, one of the poets of the new day, inferior in verse, but great in faith. It was written for New Year's Day, 1910.

Each man is captain of his soul,
And each man his own crew,
And the Pilot knows the unknown seas,
And He will bring us through.
We break new seas to-day,—
Our eager keels quest unaccustomed waters,
And, from the vast uncharted waste in front,
The mystic circles leap
To greet our prows with mightiest possibilities:
Bringing us—what?
   —Dread shoals and shifting banks,
   And calms and storms,
   And clouds and biting gales,
   And wreck and loss,
   And valiant fighting times?
And, maybe death!—and so, the **Larger Life!**

   For should the Pilot deem it best
   To cut the voyage short,
   He sees beyond the skyline, and
   He'll bring us into Port.

And, maybe, life,—life on a bounding tide,
   And chance of glorious deeds;
   —Of help swift-borne to drowning mariners,
   Of cheer to ships dismasted in the gale,
   Of succours given unasked and joyfully,
   Of mighty service to all needy souls.

   So,—Ho for the Pilot's orders,
   Whatever course He makes!
   For He sees beyond the sky line,
   And He never makes mistakes.

And, maybe, Golden Days,
   Full-freighted with delight!
   —And wide, free seas of unimagined bliss,
   And Treasure-Isles and kingdoms to be won,
   And Undiscovered Countries and new kin.

For each man captains his own soul,
And chooses his own crew,
But the Pilot knows the unknown seas,
And He will bring us through.

The other poets of whom I must briefly speak, John Davidson and James Thomson, did not live out half their days. They had genuine gifts of the poet and they began life with fair hopes and beautiful promise, but the days darkened round them and they went fast glooming to the end.

III

John Davidson (1857-1909) has many volumes of poems and plays to his name. He was the son of a Scotch minister, nurtured on porridge and poverty, who was put to work at thirteen, finally returned to school and became a pupil teacher, at last followed his demon, turned to literature, and to London as the center of life and art, voiced his many visions and experiences of joy and sorrow, and was overwhelmed by the forces he voiced but could not master. "Fleet Street Eclogues," First and Second Series, are the best known of his many volumes, poems patterned after Spenser's "Shepherd's Calendar." They are full of poetic and even fantastic contrasts, dark questionings of the meanings of life, pathetic pictures of social failure and wretchedness with idyllic touches of English scenery and life and the spirit of joyous abandon and hope. The eclogue on "St. George's Day" will give the pathetic and fantastic contrast of song and sorrow, the beauty of the English landscape and the foul ugliness of want and sin.

Of the earlier poems, Mr. Richard LeGallienne, the English poet and critic now living in New York, said in 1894, "Mr. Davidson is a personality as well as a poet. Take up any one of his books and before you have had time to differentiate its qualities, you are aware of a masculine authoritative presence. There is a burliness of constitution underlying his most delicate fanciful work. Its beauty is that best beauty which is the blossom of robust deep-rooted health; and its sweetness is that sweetness which is hived in the hearts of strong men. . . . We never lose faith in the promised land to which in the form of a magnum opus I have no doubt Mr. Davidson is leading us." These are appreciative words and thoroughly capable and honest. But John Davidson never entered the promised land predicted; he literally died in the desert. He was a man of the finest feeling and humanity: he was deeply and sorely touched by the feeling of human burdens and infirmities, but he stood alone where he could not see or help the fairer structure building,—he could only see the scaffolding and hear the cries of the workmen and be choked with the dust that filled the air.

I think he has drawn a true portrait of himself in "A Ballad in Blank Verse."

No creed for me! I am a man apart:
A mouth piece for the creeds of all the world;
A soulless life that angels may possess
Or demons haunt, wherein the foulest things
May loll at ease beside the loveliest;
A martyr for all mundane moods to tear;
The slave of every passion; and the slave
Of heat and cold, of darkness and of light;
A trembling lyre for every wind to sound.

All of Davidson's poems are of marked individuality and realism, but the later poems grew more philosophical and social and were tinged with a gloomy pessimism. His spirit is expressed in the Eclogue, "All Hallows Eve":

> In Elfland is no rest,
> But rumour and stir and endless woe
> Of the unfulfilled behest—
> The doleful yoke of the Elfinfolk
> Since first the sun went west.
>
> The cates they eat and the wine they drink,
> Savourless nothings are;
> The hopes they cherish, the thoughts they think
> Are neither near nor far;
> And well they know they cannot go
> Even to a desert star;
>
> One planet is all their poor estate,
> Though a million systems roll;
> They are dogged and worried, early and late,
> As the demons nag a soul,
> By the moon and the sun, for they never can shun
> Time's tyrannous control.

The promise of his youth did not seem fulfilled by his manhood and he fell into great poverty and mental depression and finally in 1909 he took his own life. He disappeared, and an unpublished volume of poems was found in his room, "Fleet Street Poems," with a note, "This will be my last book." The body was found several weeks after on the shore of the North Sea.

IV

James Thomson (1834-1882), author of "The City of Dreadful Night," is doubtless the most tragic figure in our recent poetry. He was a waif; he never knew his own parents, and he seemed like a bit of driftwood on the stream of life. He was brought up in the Caledonian Asylum at Glasgow, became an army teacher and was finally dismissed for breach of discipline. He was associated with Charles Bradlaugh in his secularist teachings, and in such periodicals he found his first literary work. He had no faith in religious truth, in God, the soul, and immortality. He was deeply pessimistic as regards life, under black depression concerning himself, a dipsomaniac, and died in great poverty and misery. George Meredith thinks that the taking away of poverty from his burdens would in all likelihood have saved him. He speaks of his brave heart, and says that "he had, almost past example in my experience, the thrill of the worship of valiancy as well as of sensuous beauty." And again he says: "He was a man of big heart, of such entire sincereness that he wrote directly from the impressions carved in him by his desolate experience of life. Nothing is figured; all is positive. No Inferno could be darker. But the poetical effect of a great part of the poems is that of a litany of the vaults below." (Letters, ii. 437.)

It is certain that the work of James Thomson cannot be omitted in any study of the message of modern English poetry. The poems are noteworthy for their gloomy power. The gloom pervades "Master Tenebrarum," lighted up with the faintest ray of hope, the love of a pure and gentle and beautiful soul. Had that ray of love only been followed, it might have led as in the case of Tennyson to the "ineffable light." The poem "Night" suggests the lines of Tennyson,

> An infant crying in the night
> And with no language but a cry—

only this is a man's cry who has lost his way in the impenetrable night.

In the fourteenth poem of "The City of Dreadful Night" we have the climax of the sad sincerity and tragic pathos of Thomson's unbelief,—the great cathedral, the waiting throng, the message from its pulpit,— no faith, no worship, no God.

> Who know we shall not reach the promised land;
> Perhaps a mirage glistening through our tears.
>
> *　　　*　　　*　　　*　　　*
>
> But if it prove a mirage after all!
> Our last illusion leaves us wholly bare,
> To bruise against fate's adamantine wall,
> Consumed or frozen in the pitiless air;
> In all our world, beneath, around, above,
> Our only refuge, solace, triumph,—Love,
> Sole star of light in infinite black despair.

Matthew Arnold's artistic expression of an age-tendency was Thomson's settled and fixed despair.   It was

> The sense that every struggle brings defeat
> Because fate holds no prize to crown success;
> That all the oracles are dumb or cheat
> Because they have no secret to express;
> That none can pierce the vast black veil uncertain
> Because there is no light beyond the curtain;
> That all is vanity and nothingness.

It is a sad world we have been passing through, and yet it cannot be to us what it was to Thomson; for we know that outside there is a world of light.

CHAPTER X

Poets of the Dawn

CHAPTER X

POETS OF THE DAWN

In the last chapter, it was a sad and uncertain world in which we were traveling, however sincere,—the night with feeble starlight, in which it was hard to find the way. But the soul of man cannot long live on negations. No creative impulses of imagination can come to a life flat along the earth, with no ladder reaching heavenward on which angels of God ascend and descend. The study of English poetry only confirms the optimism of Browning,—

> My own hope is, a sun will pierce
> The thickest cloud earth ever stretched;
> That, after last, returns the first,
> Though a wide compass round be fetched;
> That what began best, can't end worst,
> Nor what God blest once, prove accurst.
>
> ("Apparent Failure")

Slowly the faint light grows until color suffuses the dawn, and the day is at hand.

I

William Watson might be called the poet of the early dawn, the twilight dawn. He is something of a critic of life. He still has the questioning spirit of Arnold and Clough, and something of their persistent melancholy, but in his best moments with far more courage and hope. It is the prophecy of day. It is the turn of the tide, to change the figure. With Henley and Davidson and Thomson, you heard "its melancholy, long, withdrawing roar." Life was like the naked shingles of the world. Life seemed to have "Nor certitude, nor peace, nor help for pain." But now the sea of faith turns, and once more it shall be at the full, and men like seaweed on its sands shall drink in its life-giving food.

William Watson is never in love with melody alone; he must have serious and high thought, but the thought is held so strongly as to make simple and natural verse its inevitable form. The serious grappling with problems, the effort to interpret life does not lessen, but makes more essential the music of verse. He never, like Browning, loses the poet in the philosopher. He has not the varied music of Alfred Noyes, but he has wonderful power of phrase, etching a portrait with the fewest strokes, a condensed but vivid interpretation of character. That's the test of the real artist, not another word needed or a different word possible. That's where the best of English writers excel us: they use one word where we are tempted to use a score.

Only Sir Henry Newbolt can surpass Watson in vivid condensation. Could anything be truer or more complete than this characterization of Shelley, in a single stanza:

Impatient of the world's fixed way,
He ne'er could suffer God's delay,

But all the future in a day
  Would build divine,
And the whole past in ruins lay,
  An emptied shrine.

And the influence of Wordsworth he has drawn in
briefest lines:

Rest! 'twas the gift he gave: and peace! the shade
He spread, for spirits fevered with the sun.

There is a bit of self-revelation in the lines to Edward
Dowden (on receiving the life of Shelley), and we see
how Watson passed through periods of passion and
melody to the simple and pure beauty of spiritual vision.
He speaks first of Shelley, then of Keats and finally of
his real master Wordsworth.

In my young days of fervid poesy
He drew me to him with his strange, far light,—
He held me in a world all clouds and gleams,
And vasty phantoms, where ev'n man himself
Moved like a phantom 'mid the clouds and gleams.
Anon the earth recalled me, and a voice
Murmuring of dethroned divinities,
And dead times deathless upon sculptured urn—
And Philomela's long-descended pain
Flooding the night—and maidens of romance
To whom asleep St. Agnes' love-dreams come—
Awhile constrained me to a sweet duresse
And thraldom, lapping me in high content,
Soft as the bondage of white amorous arms.
And then a third voice, long unheeded—held
Claustral and cold, and dissonant and tame—
Found me at last with ears to hear. It sang
Of lowly sorrows and familiar joys,
Of simple manhood, artless womanhood,

And childhood fragrant as the limpid morn;
And from the homely matter nigh at hand
Ascending and dilating, it disclosed
Spaces and avenues, calm heights and breadths
Of vision, whence I saw each blade of grass
With roots that groped about eternity,
And in each drop of dew upon each blade
The mirror of the inseparable All.
The first voice, then the second, in their turns
Had sung me captive. This voice sang me free.
Therefore, above all vocal sons of men,
Since him whose sightless eyes saw hell and heaven,
To Wordsworth be my homage, thanks, and love.

Though the mind of Watson often questions, the heart is inclined to choose the best.

The grace of friendship—mind and heart
Linked with their fellow heart and mind;
The gains of science, gifts of art;
The sense of oneness with our kind;
The thirst to know and understand—
A large and liberal discontent;
These are the goods in life's rich hand,
The things that are more excellent.

    *   *   *   *   *

Though dark, O God, thy course and track,
I think Thou must at least have meant
That naught which lives should wholly lack
The things that are more excellent.

He is not content with doubt. If he cannot believe, it lessens the joy of the feast. There is an apparition behind the festal glow—

And ah, to know not, while with friends I sit,
   And while the purple joy is passed about,
Whether 'tis ampler day divinelier lit
   Or homeless night without;

And whether, stepping forth, my soul shall see
   New prospects, or fall sheer—a blinded thing!
There is, O grave, thy hourly victory,
   And there, O death, thy sting.

                      ("The Great Misgiving")

He has moments when his spirit attains to something
like *faith*. He feels the divine renewal of the earth
and would mingle his own note with the glad song of
the Spring.

I too have come through wintry terrors,—yea,
Through tempest and through cataclysm of soul
Have come, and am delivered. Me the Spring,
Me also, dimly with new life hath touched,
And with regenerate hope, the salt of life;
And I would dedicate these thankful tears
To whatsoever Power beneficent,
Veiled though his countenance, undivulged his thought,
Hath led me from the haunted darkness forth
Into the gracious air and vernal morn,
And suffers me to know my spirit a note
Of this great chorus, one with bird and stream
And voiceful mountain,—nay, a string, how jarred
And all but broken! of that lyre of life
Whereon himself, the master harp-player,
Resolving all its mortal dissonance
To one immortal and most perfect strain,
Harps without pause, building with song the world.

                            ("Vita Nuova")

Watson, like all the younger poets, has the vision of a fairer, juster world than we now know.

> The New Age stands as yet
> Half built against the sky,
> Open to every threat
> Of storms that clamor by;
> Scaffolding veils the walls,
> And dim dust floats and falls,
> As moving to and fro, their tasks the masons ply.

He has the spirit and hope of the new democracy, and holds that religion is only the mummery of priests, if it fails to heal the open sores of the world. Take the "Thoughts on Revisiting a Centre of Commerce where a Vast Cathedral Church is being Erected" (he refers to the Cathedral of St. John the Divine in New York City):

> City of merchants, lords of trade and gold,
> Traffickers great as they that bought and sold
> When ships of Tarshish came to Tyre of old;
> City of festering streets by misery trod,
> Where half-fed, half-clad children swarm unshod,
> While thou dost rear thy splendid fane to God.
> O rich in fruits and grains and oils and ores,
> And all things that the feastful earth outpours,
> Yet lacking leech-craft for thy leprous sores!
> Heal thee betimes, and cleanse thee, lest in ire
> He whom thou mock'st with pomp of arch and spire
> Come on thee sleeping, with a scythe of fire.
> Let nave and transept rest awhile; but when
> Thou hast done His work who lived and died for men,
> Then build His temple on high,—not, not, till then.

William Watson has hardly attained the promise of his early work. At times his mind has been somewhat disturbed, which may partly account for it. He has often struck a brave, true note, lent his voice to the song that is building the world. And for this we are grateful. But how can the poet reach the best and highest without the joy of a splendid vision! To Watson the light is often only twilight gray, and the way is uncertain.

> I wandered far in the wold,
> And after the heat and glare
> I came at eve to a Churchyard old:
> The yew trees seemed at prayer.
>
> And around me was dust in dust,
> And the fleeting light, and Repose—
> And the infinite pathos of human trust
> In a God whom no man knows.
> ("The Church in the Wold")

II

In Stephen Phillips we have a poet of surer note, if not so great a gift as Watson. On the appearance of his first volume, he was hailed as a poet of great promise, and that year 1897, it was crowned by the London Academy. He was a very young man then. He showed an original and musical gift, but his chief interest was in human life, not hesitating to question its deeper and more tragic phases, and tracing, to use a phrase of John Fiske, the law of love and sacrifice down into the lowest roots and crannies of the world.

No book of lyrics has appeared since the first thin volume. The last years of his life were devoted to the drama. "The Sin of David," "Francesca and Paolo,"

"Nero," "Faust," "Herod," indicate the tragic themes he has dealt with, the development of character under temptation, the awakening of the soul, its pain and growth, its defeat and triumph under sin. It is a real world he treats, the mystery of sin, the forces that live in our lives and help to shape our course that we cannot measure and so dimly understand. Yet there is no deceitful glamour over sin, no seductive music to charm and lull the soul. The destiny of man is in his own hands.

Mr. Phillips is never lawless in the treatment of the primal passions, but he is not timid and conventional. He has something of the sturdy courage and optimism of Browning:

> God never is dishonored in the spark
> He gave us from the fire of fires, and bade
> Remember whence it sprang, nor be afraid
> While that burns on, though all the rest grow dark.
> ("Any Wife to Any Husband")

I remember that some of his early poems were severely criticized by a writer in the *Athenæum,* as dealing with subjects too coarse, subjects that were beneath poetry. "The Woman with the Dead Soul" was one of them. What interest could we have, asked the writer, in a poor serving woman whose soul burned and flickered and went out through drudgery and the street! And there was the wife who sold her body to buy bread for her husband sick and starving through out of work. What nobleness and ideality could there be in such vulgar scenes? It was not poetry for cultivated souls; it was the verse of the slum! But this, I think, is not condemnation but high praise. It is the nobility of Stephen Phillips that he is not exclusive, the pet of the

club or the drawing-room, but the brother of the poor,
the friend of the unfortunate, that he can feel with the
lowly and interpret the heart that struggles and suffers
amid shame and defeat. It is a true realism, a life
which only the poet can see in its tragic import, and
present so that it shall be cleansing of social pride and
cruelty and work for a day when society shall not be
built on the sorrows and sins of the poor.

There is the beauty and power of true pathos in the
picture of the wife who had vainly made the sacrificial
offering of herself for bread.

> She felt how cold is God, how brief our breath,
> How vain is any love, how strong is death;
> O fool, O fool! to have so quickly died;
> I am unclean forevermore, she cried;
> And then with fear, with gathering distrust,
> Swiftly between his teeth the morsels thrust.
> Then stiller grew; and with a moaning slow
> Relented now, and wearied in her woe.
> But as the woman, dying in her thought,
> Looked upward; at her dress her baby caught,
> And she revived, and toward her little son
> Ventured, that he into her arms might run.
> And like a strange woman all doubtfully
> She stretched her arms out, shining wistfully,
> As though with meek advances she beguiled
> Into her sighing bosom her own child.
> Then pulled him close to her, and held him there,
> And those tears fell down into his hair.
> Softly she said: "O cruel new-born thing!
> The years to you a gentleness will bring:
> Then think of me as one that not in thought,
> But out of yearning into woe was brought."
> So as she mourned above him, the old farm
> With evening noises in the twilight charm

Returned, and she remembered quiet trees
Just stirring; she can hear the very breeze!
Her prudent mother wisely to her speaks,
Her peaceful hair a little sorrow streaks.
And as a soft and dreadful summer day
Will suddenly through chill December stray,
So the mild beauty of old happiness
Wandered into her mind with strange distress;
Till slowly with the gathering light, lo life
Came back to her; desire and dust and strife;
The huge and various world with murmur grand.

Through the strong and tender humanity of Stephen
Phillips runs a faith in a better world than this and in
a Divine power that wills and is working for it.
"Lazarus," with perhaps a memory of Browning's "Letter of Ben Karshish," expresses the reverent love for
the Friend of Man, the Lord of Life.

O face that seemest made to weep and smile
With us, and hands all rough with common tasks!
Is this, indeed, thy sun to which Thou hast
Recalled me, and are these Thy fields, which grow
Slowly from gray to green before my eyes?
I felt Thee irresistible in the grave.
Forgive me that I talked so lightly, and went
So unconcerned beside Thee in old days.
How is it Thou canst care to come and go
With such as me, and walk and work with us,
Thou at whose whisper Death idled and grieved,
And knew the voice at which creation shone
Suddenly? Yet was I so near to peace:
And I came back to life remorsefully,
When the sea murmured again, and fields appeared.
But how should I complain? Unto what end
I am recalled I know not; but if Thou
Art here content to be, then why not I?

And there is the true expression of faith, pressed out of his human love and need, in his attitude towards personal loss and sorrow.

> Thou power, that beyond the wind
> Rulest, to Thee I am resigned.
> My child from me is snatched away:
> She vanished at the peer of day.
> Yet I discern with clearer brow
> A high indulgence in the blow,
> Light in the storm that o'er me broke,
> A special kindness in the stroke,
> A gentleness behind the law,
> A sweetness following on the awe.
> Shall I forget that noon-day hour,
> When as upon some favorite flower
> A deep and tingling bliss was shed,
> A thrilling peace from overhead?
> I had not known it since my birth,
> I shall not know it more on earth.
> But now I may not sin, nor err,
> For fear of ever losing her.
> Though reeling from Thy thunder-blow,
> Though blinded with Thy lightning low,
> I stagger back to dismal life,
> And mix myself with mortal strife,
> Thy judgment still to me is sweet;
> I feel, I feel, that we must meet.

Surely I am right in calling Stephen Phillips a poet of the growing light, reverent towards God and sensitive to all human need.

III

Two other poets have something in common, in their simple and vivid realities and broad sympathies and their bold originality. I refer to Wilfrid Wilson Gibson and John Masefield.

You may not think that Mr. Gibson stands for growing light. I do not know that he has a positive religious tone. It may seem like turning back after Stephen Phillips. But I think he contributes to faith, faith in man at least. Like a true artist, he can touch a scene of human passions with ideal light and yet not take away any of its reality. He can deal with the most hopeless scenes of human life yet lose no heart. There is no bitterness in him, no cynical pessimism. His wholesome nature interprets for him the essential worth of life.

Mr. Gibson has the art of interpreting life and natural scenery in the most delicate yet vivid way. "The Gorse" can hardly be surpassed for the combined realism of man and nature, the fear of a hunted man "stung to headlong flight."

> He blundered towards the league-wide yellow blaze,
> "Bewildered in a glittering golden maze
>   Of stinging scented fire."

And he interprets loss in the same subtle art; some simple fact of nature giving voice to the soul's bereavement.

> We who are left, how shall we look again
> Happily on the sun or feel the rain
> Without remembering how they who went
> Ungrudgingly and spent
> Their lives for us loved, too, the sun and rain?
> A bird among the rain-wet lilac sings—
> But we, how shall we turn to little things

And listen to the birds and winds and streams
Made holy by their dreams,
Nor feel the heart-break in the heart of things.

("Lament")

But I think Mr. Gibson's most significant work is found in "Daily Bread." The book is made up of sketches of the English poor in the form of single act plays. The characters in each are few, and they stand out with the distinctness of real life. Some moment is chosen when the light falls upon the bareness of their lot, the frame-wasting drudgery, the risk of toil, the slow starvation, the sturdy hands stretched out in vain for work, the pathos of broken hopes. Yet through it all is the essential worth of life, the heroism of simple duty, the life that time nor choice can weaken nor destroy.

The first-born is taken, and the mother says:

My bosom yearns for him.
Your heart will evermore be empty.

And the husband replies:

Nay, wife, nay!
Shall not your breast and mine
Be ever full of love for him?
Sweet memories of him
Shall nestle in our hearts,
Forevermore.
And we have still each other.

And the mother adds,

And our son!

An old woman whose youngest and last son has been taken by the toil of the sea, exclaims:

> I have not found much happiness in life;
> And now all that I've toiled for,
> The happiness I thought within my reach,
> That I have labored after all these years,
> Is snatched from me;
> And in the end,
> I find no balm of peace.
> And still have I not toiled?
> And toil is something more than happiness;
> 'Tis life itself.
> I have not flinched from life
> But looked it in the face.
>
> ("The Betrothed")

Mr. Gibson well says of such scenes:

> All life moving to one measure—
> Daily bread, daily bread—
> Bread of life, and bread of labor,
> Bread of bitterness and sorrow,
> Hand-to-mouth, and no to-morrow,
> Death for house mate, death for neighbor—
> Yet when all the babes are fed,
> Love, are there not crumbs to treasure?

Mr. Gibson has written much since the first volume. Poems have been collected under the title, "Borderlands and Thoroughfares," and his poems are frequently found in our best monthlies. He has large interests, sees the significant elements in a scene or experience, has vivid description of nature and vital interpretation of life. But the first book "Daily Bread" is characteristic and prophetic of the man. Behind rough faces and in hard conditions, he sees the essential worth of man. His verse is always charged with human interest and feeling.

IV

John Masefield is proof that poetry is the gift of the gods and not of the schools. The schools have had nothing to do with it. "The poet is born, not made." Tennyson could not attain his greatness without the schools, that fine culture of the university, that study of the great thinkers of the world, that intercourse with refined and noble minds, the mastery of the materials and laws of his art. He could not have been Tennyson without all this. It made him a Master, and all others of the time are indebted to him.

But Masefield without any adventitious aids, without the help of institutions and literatures and men seems destined to a place in English literature hardly second to Tennyson. He is only in middle life. And almost every year, notable work comes from him, flows like the waters of a great spring in the mountains down into the valleys.

He is the product of the race and not of any special environment or culture, like Shakspere or Burns, like Bunyan or Spurgeon, like John Bright or John Burns. He not only rises from the common stock like some wild flower or fruit from the earth; but his experience has been so strange and varied that nature and life speak with wonderful realism in his verse, and he has something of a universal note.

Masefield has been a sailor before the mast and in many seas; he has followed the herds over the vast and unconquered pampas of Argentine, that land so inconceivable to us, and yet made real by Hudson, the English naturalist; he has stood behind the bar in a New York saloon, a student of the underworld; he took many a handy turn in the great war; and everywhere, scene, event, person made their impress on the sensitive plate of his genius.

He is our chief narrator. He writes as good prose as verse. You will find no better yarns of the fo'castle than a "Tarpaulin Muster." Yet his gift is in narrative poetry. The herder's life, the vast and monotonous pastures of the Argentine, and life common and romantic and tragic are all in "The Daffodil Fields." There couldn't be a greater contrast than "Reynard the Fox" and "Right Royal," the recent books depicting an English hunt and a steeple chase. The ceaseless motion, the intense, excited strivings, the terrible hazards, the final excitement, it does not seem possible that poetry could narrate it all, and yet be poetry; the ever new symbolism, the accuracy of scene, the human spirit and the animal venture, the horse and rider in oneness of striving,—such sustained narrative has not been equalled since Sir Walter Scott. I quote from a criticism in a recent *Yale Review*: "Masefield has made himself beyond any living poet the voice of great English traditions speaking in the modern world. In him survives the devout chivalry of Chaucer's 'Book of the Duchess,' Spenser's Platonic enthusiasm for ideal beauty, the valiancy of Elizabethan adventurers and Shakspere's heroes, a passionate tenderness for the ancient countryside, and an almost unspeakable love for tall ships and the sea. His 'Reynard the Fox' and this glorification of the steeple chase 'Right Royal' are great poems of English sport; one can hardly imagine a time when Englishmen will not love them, or when they will not

be the classical treatment of steeple-chasing and fox-
hunting. But they are much more than sporting poems.
Masefield with his deeply traditional genius has sat-
urated his themes with historical feeling, and made
them true episodes in the epic of the English race."
(April, 1921.)

But I do not forget the purpose of this study. Has
Masefield a spiritual message? He began as a writer
of plays, but best expresses himself in narrative lyrics.

The "Everlasting Mercy" is called "the most daring,
realistic, and beautiful poetry that has been written for
a great while," and it received the prize of the London
Academy for the best literary work of the year. It is
certainly daring and realistic. It is a bold man who
would find poetry in a prize fight, an unchaste bar-
maid and a brute crazed by drink. It is so realistic
that you cannot read parts of it aloud, and you almost
blush to read it in the privacy of your own room. It's
like going with a police detective to see the underworld.
And you do see it, and you can hardly draw breath in
that foul air. The poem has atmosphere. There is no
doubt of that. Hogarth's drawings are not more realistic.

Your first thought is a question whether such scenes
can be poetry. You call to mind Stopford Brooke's
criticism of the spasmodic school, the group of "hot-
tempered, passionate, egotistic" young poets. (Oscar
Wilde and that set.) "The senses, the appetites are
part of human nature. They also are to be presented
in poetry; but then, if art represents their base ex-
tremes, such art has ceased to be art, and has passed
into the science of morbid conditions." But you soon
feel that the wonderful realism of ruffianism and de-
bauchery are that we may measure the true recovery

of the soul, and understand in part the redeeming power
of the "Everlasting Mercy." It is Harold Begbie with
a poet's soul. How can we know the miracle of the
lily without the black earth from which it grew!

> O lovely lily clean,
> O lily springing green,
> O lily bursting white,
> Dear lily of delight,
> Spring in my heart again
> That I may flower to men.

The poem also has a social message. It is an exact
picture of the brutality and lewdness that center in the
public house of many an English village. And the
frenzied man's accusation of the parson and the squire
has enough truth in it to waken consciences that slumber under a traditional system.

And it has scenes of simple and exquisite beauty.
And the redeemed drunkard's delight in nature is only
what John Bunyan felt when he called upon the birds
to join with him in the new song.

> So up the road I wander slow
> Past where the snow-drops used to grow
> With celandines in early springs,
> When rainbows were triumphant things
> And dew so bright and flowers so glad,
> Eternal joy to lass and lad.
> And past the lovely brook I paced,
> The brook whose source I never traced,
> The brook, the one of two which rise
> In my green dream of Paradise,
> In wells where heavenly buckets clink
> To give God's wandering thirsty drink
> By those clean cots of carven stone

Where the clear water sings alone.
Then down, past that white-blossomed pond,
And past the chestnut trees beyond,
And past the bridge the fishers knew,
Where yellow flag flowers once grew,
Where we'd go gathering cops of clover,
In Sunny June times long since over.
O clover-cops half white, half red,
O beauty from beyond the dead.
O blossom, key to earth and heaven,
O souls that Christ has new forgiven.

The late President Hyde of Bowdoin College calls
Masefield our most effective modern preacher of the
exceeding sinfulness of sin, its meanness and wanton-
ness and cruelty. And he takes "The Widow in the
Bye Street" as the text for the meanness of sin. As
Dickens shows Steerforth the Seducer in the light of
the grief of the Peggoty household, so John Masefield
shows sexual sin against the background of the misled
boy's broken-hearted mother. And that's where you
must see it to know how cruel and contemptible it is.
It is sin against motherhood. It always breaks some
mother's heart.

And there are few passages of modern poetry so
profoundly religious as the prayer of the mother at the
execution of her misguided son.

"And God who gave His mercies takes His mercies,
And God who gives beginning gives the end.
I dread my death; but it's the end of curses,
A rest for broken things too broke to mend.
O Captain Christ, our blessed Lord and Friend,
We are two wandered sinners in the mire,
Burn our dead hearts with love out of Thy fire.

And when thy death comes, Master, let us bear it
As of Thy will, however hard to go;
Thy Cross is infinite for us to share it,
Thy help is infinite for us to know.
And when the long trumpets of the Judgment blow
May our poor souls be glad and meet agen,
And rest in Thee." "Say, 'Amen,' Jim." "Amen."

Mr. Masefield has seen much of life. He has had
the wanderlust of many a young Englishman. But out
of his vagabondage he has come purified of many foolish notions, with calmness of vision and with profound
understanding and pity for men in their conflicting
desires. He has finely given his own philosophy of life,
drawn from his checkered experiences.

The many-pictured world of many passions
Wears out the nations as a woman's fashions,
And what life is is much to very few;
Men being so strange, so mad, and what men do
So good to match or share; but when men count
Those hours of life that were a bursting fount,
Sparkling the dusty heart with living springs,
There seems a world, beyond our earthly things,
Gated by golden moments, each bright time
Opening to show the city white like lime,
High-towered and many-peopled. This made sure,
Work that obscures those moments seems impure,
Making our not-returning time of breath
Dull with the ritual and records of death,
That frost of fact by which our wisdom gives
Correctly stated death to all that lives.

Best trust the happy moments. What they give
Makes man less fearful of the certain grave,
And gives his work compassion and new eyes.
The days that make us happy make us wise.

I have called the group of men we have considered in this chapter, Poets of the Dawn. It may seem an uncertain light to some of you. The morning is gray with clouds, and storms still sweep the sky. But the morning has dawned. A new day has come.

CHAPTER XI

Poets of the New Day

CHAPTER XI

POETS OF THE NEW DAY

There is a deep impression voiced in many ways, that we are at the beginning of another creative era in poetry. The opening of the nineteenth century was such an era, only matched once before in the history of our language, "the spacious times of great Elizabeth." The forces then, scientific, democratic, religious, stirred the national life, and found their finest expression and their most pervasive influence in a group of great poets.

Similar forces are troubling the depths of our life to-day. The scientific spirit has passed from its critical phase into constructive ideals that have quickened and enlarged every realm of thought and endeavor. The democratic movement has broadened and deepened with the century until it is not the struggle for political rights against the power of a few, but the effort to give the downmost man a soul, to open to all a human way of life. And it is world-wide. The world war made the democratic movement evident and dominant; in the sententious language of the Chicago *Tribune,* "It is the twilight of the Kings. Western Democracy of the people marches eastward." And in spite of terrible reactions, the cynical pessimism that followed the heights of sacrifice, in every nation are groups of idealists who have vowed to make war accursed, and at whatever cost to be true to their visions of a just and humane world.

And religion as never before is the question of universal life; its questions not battled for so much in the upper air as on the earth where men sin and suffer, struggle and hope. The scientific spirit and the democratic movement have both helped to the conception of God in his world of nature and human life, have humanized religion, and carried it into every sphere and province of man's life.

The poets feel and index this new life. Their strings vibrate with the faintest breath of the Spirit. The poets tell of Spring before the buds swell or the first robins come. One robin doesn't make a summer, but when a small flock of robins is hopping over our lawns, and singing in our trees, we know that May "with one great gust of blossom" will soon storm our world.

The poets have come. They have felt the breath of the new life and they are singing its message. We may call them minor poets; we do not know what some of them may become. It would be easy to count two score in England who give the accent of the deeper life. There may be as many in our own land, though they are hardly heard in the din of our machinery or the bustling importance of our politics.

One of our weekly reviews recently referred to the significant fact that two magazines of poetry have been started in America: *Poetry* in Chicago and the *Poetry Journal* in Boston. And the latter quotes from Professor Woodberry of Columbia to show the relation between poetry and the national life: "The notion that poetry is a thing remote from life is a singular delusion; it is more truly to be described as the highway of our days, though we tread it, as children tread the path of innocence, without knowing it. Nothing is more constant in the life of boy or man than the outgoing of his soul into the world about him, and this outgoing, however it be achieved, is the act of poetry." And Mr. Hamilton Mabie says of the new English poetry, "It is well worth studying . . . because it shows that the soul of the country is awake. It is clean poetry; it has not fallen into the slough of eroticism which dulls the senses, blurs the vision, and blights the imagination. One feels in it the passion for humanity which heralds a rebirth of freedom in the modern world. Much of it is crude, but so are all beginnings. It must not be overpraised, but it ought to be recognized. The people who do not know their poets have ceased to hear the voices of their own souls."

I think the most significant fact of the new poetry is its changed attitude towards religion. The great poets of every age are religious. They view life as a whole and that whole is incomprehensible without God. But lesser minds do not rise above the mists that settle down upon an age. After Tennyson and Browning was a school of true poets but men of feebler light and feeling, to whom Christian truth was a superstition or a perhaps. Swinburne, Rossetti, Morris, Meredith were not irreligious, but critical towards the creeds and institutions of the Christian Church, regarding them as simply the development of the religious spirit of man, often unrational, or as the institutions of an old order, hostile to the highest rational and social growth. And there were not a few that made poetry a sensuous and esthetic delight, or the fierce cry of a baffled and despairing spirit.

But there is little of the discordant and defiant note of a storm and stress period in the younger poets. If there are problems that baffle the understanding, there is brave work to do and light enough to catch something of its meaning and the divine event to which all is moving. If religious faith is not always pronounced, the heart still questioning, it is the quest of hope, and prophetic of the day when the mountain peaks shall be bathed in the light, though the shadows linger in the lower vales.

Our modern life has been stirred to its deepest depths by the shock of forces long gathering. Where no nation has clean hands, it is folly to attempt to fix the final guilt for the contest that has brought our civilization to the brink of ruin. But through the confused alarms of war, one truth is clear to the Christian seer: the war is only a colossal phase of the eternal contest between old systems and the living Word.

Under such trying experiences the elemental nature of man is laid bare. The breaking of old habits and precious ties, the uncertainties and perils of the days, the appeal of a cause which men associate with patriotism and the will of God, the terrible discipline of suffering, awaken the nobler powers of life and assert our kinship with God.

> There is no God, the foolish saith,
> But none, there is no sorrow.
>
> *   *   *   *   *
>
> And eyes the preacher could not school
> By wayside graves are raised,
> And lips cry "God be pitiful,"
> That ne'er said "God be praised."

The first call to sacrifice awakened latent manhood and found expression in strong religious feeling. The first months of the war the *Cologne Gazette* wrote, "The vulgar and impure are no more seen in our shop windows, nor the suggestive heard in our theaters. The

German people are thinking high thoughts." *Le Matin* of Paris said, "The Churches are once more filled, and a new honor is given to the priesthood." M. Barrès, editing the journals of young French officers, finds an elevated religious spirit. "They shall live," he exclaims, "but if they should perish, France shall be built anew with their lives, as with living stones." And the *Westminster Gazette* said, "Never since Cromwell have so many soldiers marched under the sense of Divine direction."

I know we have been wisely cautioned against placing undue hope on the emotional fervors awakened by sacrifice. War is brutal, destructive, wasteful, not only of life and treasure, but of the very fruits of the Spirit. "Do men gather grapes of thorns, or figs of thistles?" Disillusion comes from the long, grey, wasting years. "The real loss of war," says an English critic, "is loss of faith in justice, in humanity, in the soul itself."

But I am sure there is a deeper meaning than this. Even a momentary response is a revelation of the soul's capacity.

> What we long for, that we are
> For one transcendent moment.

The finest souls of the world have always been purified by fire; and there's many a touch of the unseen upon the common mind. Millions have been fairly driven to God: it has been God or dumb despair or brute indifference. Many have won their faith as Job did through deepest experience of pain and loss: "I know that my vindicator liveth."

And this deep experience has created poetry and found its noblest expression in poetry. Only poetry could voice some of its moods or catch some of its

visions. In such a world-disturbance, every life is
touched. All the well-known poets have something to
say, and unexpected voices are heard.

> Heaven flowed upon the soul in many dreams
> Of high desire.

There were no mute, inglorious Miltons. Never before did such a multitude find poetry the natural and
necessary mode of expression.

In this new poetry of war there is a remarkable
absence of the purely martial ring. It is true there are
no more thrilling war lyrics in our language. Lord
Tennyson's "Charge of the Light Brigade," or Sir
Henry Newbolt's "Lampida Vitæ" can not more stir
the blood than Campbell's "Langemarke at Ypres" or
Conan Doyle's "The Guards Came Through," or Herbert Kaufman's "The Hell Gate of Soissons." But in
this poetry there is no glory in war itself, no cruel lust
of conquest. We are reminded of the word of the
noble French captain, "There is no glory in war; the
glory is in the soul of man." The silent sense, sometimes breaking into passionate expression, of the moral
justification of so dreadful a thing as war, the revolt
of the Christian conscience, the abhorrence and protest
of all that makes the taste and excellence of life against
the necessity of war, give the high resolve and moral
enthusiasm, the dread force to men essentially lovers
of peace.

When James Elroy Tucker strikes the note of English pride and patriotism in "The Dying Patriot"—

> Sleep not, my country, though night is here, afar
> Your children of the morning are clamorous for war;

and besides appeals to the love of the sea, and the sea-girt land:

> When they come forth to seek this empire o'er thee,
> And I go forth to meet them, on that day
> God grant to us the old Armada weather,
> The winds that rip, the heavens that stoop and lour—

the poet thinks less of the glory of the smashing blow than on the sacrificial consecration of the spirit.

It is the cleansing might of sacrifice that has awakened the noblest song as it has the most heroic character. The English language has rarely pulsed with stronger thought and feeling than in "Subalterns, a Song of Oxford," by Miss Mildred Huxley, first published in the *Spectator*.

> They had so much to lose; their radiant laughter
> Shook my old walls—how short a time ago,
> I hold the echoes of their song hereafter
> Among the precious things I used to know.
>
> Their cup of life was full to overflowing,
> All earth had laid its tribute at their feet.
> What harvest might we hope from such a sowing?
> What noonday from a dawning so complete?
>
> And I—I watched them working, dreaming, playing,
> Saw their young bodies fit the mind's desire,
> Felt them reach outward, upward, still obeying
> The passionate dictates of their hidden fire.
>
> Yet here and there some grey-beard breathed derision,
> 'Too much of luxury, too soft an age!
> Your careless Galahads will see no vision,
> Your knights will make no mark on honor's page.'

No mark? Go ask the broken fields in Flanders,
Ask the great dead who watch, in ancient Troy,
Ask the old moon as round the world she wanders,
What of the men who were my hope and joy!

They are but fragments of Imperial splendor,
Handfuls of might amidst a mighty host,
Yet I, who saw them go with proud surrender,
May surely claim to love them first and most.

They who had all, gave all. Their half-writ story
Lies in the empty halls they knew so well,
But they, the knights of God, shall see His glory,
And find the Grail ev'n in the fire of hell.

And this brings us to the starred name—suggesting
the incalculable loss of war,—the gifted young poet,
the modern Byron but a nobler Byron, once known as
a careless Bohemian, a clever verse-maker, who became in the white light of patriotism and valor, "a
poet whom it is not absurd to call great." Let Rupert
Brooke himself tell the secret of his spiritual awakening:

Blow, bugles, blow! They brought us for our dearth
Holiness lacked so long, and love and pain.
Honor has come back as a king to earth,
And paid his subjects with a royal wage:
And nobleness walks in our ways again;
And we have come into our heritage.

We should hardly call war a school of piety. The
many are made reckless and brutal by it. A chosen
few come through the great ordeal better men. The
discipline, the imminence of death, the demand for
sympathy and sacrifice, the banner of a noble cause
awaken true self-hood, a new reverence, and idealism

and devotion. Religion is born of it, a turning to God, when every human helper fails. It is voiced again and again, notably in Alfred Noyes' "A Prayer in War Time." Christ and his cross is felt anew, if not wholly understood, as the eternal truth of God, and at the heart of human mystery. "Christ in Flanders," from an almost unknown singer, in simple, appealing lines speaks of the sin and sorrow, the struggle and pain of man as in the heart of the Eternal Father. This vicarious law of life is expressed in "The Three Hills" of Everard Owen, written from Eton:

> There is a hill in England,
> Green fields and a school I know,
> Where the balls fly fast in summer,
> And the whispering elm-trees grow;
>   A little hill, a dear hill,
>   And the playing fields below.
>
> There is a hill in Flanders,
> Heaped with a thousand slain,
> Where the shells fly night and noon-tide
> And the ghosts that died in vain,—
>   A little hill, a hard hill
>   To the souls that died in pain.
>
> There is a hill in Jewry,
> Three crosses pierce the sky,
> On the midmost He is dying
> To save all those who die,—
>   A little hill, a kind hill
>   To souls in jeopardy.

The reality of the living Christ is felt anew in such lines as Prys-Jones' "The Everlasting Arms," or in "The Faithful Comrade," by P. J. Fisher.

Where stark and shattered walls
Mourn desolate to the sky
He buildeth me a home,
And well doth fortify.

The sweeping scythes play **near**
And shrill about my head;
I look into His eyes
That smile away my dread.

And when with faltering feet
I thread the perilous trench,
His print the clay before
And shame me if I blench.

If nerve and spirit yield
Before the grim demands,
New power is in the touch
Of His transfigured hands.

The thousand barbarous **tongues**
Of war may round me brawl;
His love within my heart
Sings louder than them all.

O edgeless armament!
O empty jeopardy!
While He, my Comrade, walks
The stricken fields with me.

And the thought of the Immortal Lite has a new and
joyous significance, not through spirits that peep and
mutter, or the sentimental craving that seeks the living
among the dead, but in the multitude of young knights
who have gone West, to the adventure and service of
a new world:

Paradise now is the soldier's land,
Their own country its shining sod,

Common all in a merry band;
And the young knights' laughter pleaseth God.
(Katharine Tynan, "New Heaven")

The poets tell us that on the soul of man is the handwriting of God, and like an old palimpsest, however obscured by the marks of a selfish and faithless life, the divine message stands clear again through the sharp chemicals of suffering.

The poetry of the war is more than an incident in the awakening of imagination and feeling that promised a new day for English song. Such poetry would not have been possible without the men who stood in the succession of Chaucer and Milton, Wordsworth and Browning. It is a group of poets that justifies my theme, of whom I would especially speak. There may be forty of them, a noble group, most of their names found in the volumes of Georgian Poetry, collections made in recent years from books and from papers and reviews like the *Spectator,* the *Athenæum* and the *Nation.*

It is new poetry and yet it is marked by its reverence for the great standards of the masters. They have learned the freshness and vividness of the best free verse. They have learned the "crisp, incisive and terse" diction that deals with immediate and external impression. They know the artistic possibilities of new systems, the beauty of many an image that lends distinction to the new school; but they also know that poetry must do something more than be busied with its own craftsmanship, than enjoy its own sensations however exquisite, that there are still "exaltations, agonies, and love and man's unconquerable mind," and with these the poet must wrestle if he would be the guide and interpreter of life. The best of the new poets are not iconoclasts, cutting themselves off from the past and despising its work, but the children of the prophets, rejoicing in their heritage and trying to carry on and add to the great traditions of English song. Yet these new poets are poets of freedom. They are independent and original, never the slaves of convention; pioneers of progress, bold enough to venture beyond the old landmarks. Gordon Bottomley's Lear gives no hint of Shakspere's great creation, yet it has its own dramatic power. It is a cruder, more barbaric Lear than Shakspere's, and I am sure it is nearer to the times and manners of the early Celtic Kings. It lays bare the elemental passions with coarse but telling realism.

And James Stephen's "Lonely God" tells the story of the Lost Paradise differently from the Genesis narrative or Milton's great epic, but with a humanness that appeals to our modern thought. It harmonizes with our best thought of religion that Paradise would be a lonely place without the children, and surely it is in harmony with Christ's thought of God, the Master who sends his servants into the highways and byways, who would have all come to his feast, that his house might be full.

There is more than one modern poet that suggests the thinker. You can not get his whole message by a single careless reading. They are far more than a single lyric cry, an impressionist's picture of a single scene of nature or a single phase of life. Once more they have taken their calling seriously, to interpret life, to help men to live, to furnish noble grounds for noble emotions, to show the age to itself and be heralds of a better day. Both Abercrombie and Bottomley take the "End of the World" as a poetic theme, the first describing the effect of a blazing comet upon a coarse,

ignorant crowd of an English public house: the superstitious fear, the panic, the hasty repentance, the old
life resumed when the fear is gone; while Bottomley
pictures a single family dying of cold, the final extinc-
tion of life without the sun. The latter, in "Babel, the
Gate of God," interprets the building genius of man,
in ancient temples and towers and pyramids, as the
craving of the race after God.

> Space, the old source of time, should be undone,
> Eternity defined, by men who trusted
> Another tier would equal them with God.

Such examples show the tendency of the best modern English poetry to deal with significant themes, to
deal with great materials, and not carve statues out of
cherry stones.

There is a certain *prophetic* sense in this poetry; it
appeals to the nobler elements of men and interprets
the motives and forces that would make for spiritual
progress. Not that its themes are religious in the technical sense,—there are many fine examples of this;—
but as nature herself is a missionary, the very stones
of the field in league with righteousness, as man and
human affairs tell of a moral order and purpose, so
these poems in dealing with the greater themes of life,
in picturing the real motives and conflicts of the human
heart, speak for God and make for the higher life of
the race.

Perhaps nothing is more significant of this serious
element than the "Sale of St. Thomas" by Lascelles
Abercrombie. The poet deals with the legend of St.
Thomas and India. The Apostle stands on the dock
about to sail for the distant land. But he thinks of the
dangers of the sea.

How fearful is this trade of sailing! Worse
Than all land-evils is the water-way
Before me now.—What, cowardice? Nay, why
Trouble myself with ugly words? 'Tis prudence,
And prudence is an admirable thing.

    *   *   *   *   *

I, who have seen God, I put myself
Amid the heathen outrage of the sea
In a deal-wood box! It were plain folly.

Then Thomas thinks of the climate of India, and its
breeds of insect and reptile life, and more than all the
strange and cruel superstitions of its people, and he
shrinks from the venture.

If Christ desired India, He had sent
The band of us, solder'd in one great purpose,
To strike His message through those dark, vast tribes.
But one man!—O surely it is folly
And we misread the lot! One man, to thrust,
Even though in his soul the lamp was kindled
At God's own hands, one man's lit soul to thrust
The immense Indian darkness out of the world!

Then a noble stranger approaches the quay, the Master
in disguise, and says to the captain that this man is his
runaway slave; sells him to the captain, and gives these
parting words to his servant.

Now, Thomas, know thy sin. It was not fear;
Easily may a man crouch down for fear,
And yet rise up on firmer knees, and face
The hailing storm of the world with graver courage.
But prudence, prudence is the deadly sin,
And one that groweth deep into a life,
With hardening roots that clutch about the breast,

For this refuses faith in the unknown powers
Within man's nature, shrewdly bringeth all
Their inspiration of strange eagerness
To a judgment bought by safe experience;
Narrows desire into the scope of thought.
But it is written in the heart of man,
Thou shalt no larger be than thy desire.
Thou must not therefore stoop thy spirit's sight
To pore only within the candle-gleam
Of conscious wit and reasonable brain;
But search into the sacred darkness lying
Outside thy knowledge of thyself, the vast
Measureless fate, full of the power of stars,
The outer, noiseless heavens of thy soul.
Keep thy desire closed in the room of light
The laboring fires of thy mind have made,
And thou shalt find the vision of thy spirit
Pitifully dazzled to so shrunk a ken,
There are no spacious puissances about it.
But send desire often forth to scan
The immense night which is thy greater soul;
Knowing the possible, see thou try beyond it
Into impossible things, unlikely ends;
And thou shalt find thy knowledgeable desire
Grow large as all the regions of thy soul,
Whose firmaments doth cover the whole of Being,
And of created purpose reach the ends.

"The Fires of God," by John Drinkwater (best
known to us by his drama of Lincoln), is perhaps the
finest example of the spirit of modern poetry, in trying
to lead life, to pluck out the heart of the mystery.

A man looks at his life and confesses that he has not
really lived.

Along the ways wheredown my feet have passeo
I see the years with little triumph crowned, * * *

Poor barren years that brooded overmuch
On your own burden.

He resolves that henceforth he will live: he will try to
know life and fill out its full measure.

Henceforth my hands are lifted to the touch
Of hands that labor with me, and my heart
Hereafter to the world's heart shall be set
And its own pain forget.
Time gathers to my name,—
Days dead are dark; the days to be, a flame
Of wonder and of promise, and great cries
Of travelling people reach us,—I must rise.

But how shall a man rise to the height possible for him?
Shall he do it by the strength of his own might and
will?

Was I not man? Could I not rise alone
Above the shifting of the things that be,
Rise to the crest of all the stars, and see
The ways of all the world as from a throne?

But he could not attain life in this way. He was a
man of little vision.

Great only in unconsecrated pride.
*   *   *   *   *
So I forgot my God, and I forgot
The holy sweet communion of men.
And ever to myself I lied,
Saying, "Apart from all men thus I go
To know the things that they may never know."

Then a great change befell.

From arrogant thoughts of self, the soul turns to the
study of human life. If we cannot know God, we can
know our fellow-men. The present may be only a little
span of life, but shall we not find the secret here? But
he finds the little span of life blackened with the wing
of perilous evil, bateless misery.

> Where many a ruined grace
> And many a friendless care
> Ran to and fro in sorrowful unrest.

Again the soul confesses its failure.

> O fool, O only great
> In pride unhallowed, O most blind of heart!
> Confusion but more dark confusion bred,
> Grief nurtured grief. I cried aloud and said,
> 'Through trackless ways the soul of man is hurled,
> No sign upon the forehead of the skies,
> No beacon, and no chart,
> Are given to him, and the inscrutable world
> But mocks his scars and fills his mouth with dust.'

> And lies bore lies
> And lust bore lust,
> And the world was heavy with flowerless rods,
> And pride outran
> The strength of a man
> Who had set himself in the place of Gods.

Then from the bitter shame of spirit, the soul turns in
humble wise.

> And I beheld the fruitful earth, with store
> Of odorous treasure, full and golden grain,
> *   *   *   *   *

And the great hills and solemn chanting seas
And prodigal meadows, answering to the chime
Of God's good year.

And the message of the earth was the same message that
the second Isaiah gave to the faithless captives in
Babylon, and that Jesus gave to the doubting disciples.
And the certainty of God's word in nature gave a new
meaning to his word in human life, to all the struggle
and confusion of the years.

And then he heard a new music

that compelled,
Surrender of all tributary fears.

O blessed voices, O compassionate hands,
Calling and healing, O great-hearted brothers!
I come to you.   Ring out across the lands
Your benediction, and I too will sing
With you, and haply kindle in another's
Dark, desolate hour, the flame you stirred in me.
O bountiful earth, in adoration meet
I bow to you; O glory of years to be,
I too will labor to your fashioning.
Go down, go down, unweariable feet,
Together we will march towards the ways
Wherein the marshalled hosts of morning wait
In sleepless watch, with banners wide unfurled
Across the skies in ceremonial state,
To greet the men who lived triumphant days,
And stormed the secret beauty of the world.

John Drinkwater gives us no slight, ephemeral beauty,
but the abiding beauty of truth.   And this is poetry, not
some idle fancy of an hour, but life in its deepest

meaning and noblest aspect. As long as men love and suffer and aspire, as long as there is search for truth and the craving for perfection, the poets will be the true prophets of the race. Not until "mankind is dead and the world cold," to use the words of Bottomley in his "Atlantis," "Poetry's immortality will pass."

One name remains to be discussed and that the most positively spiritual and Christian of them all. Of course I mean Mr. Alfred Noyes. Whether his active life as writer and teacher and lecturer on both sides the sea will give him time and quiet to perfect his art and see life whole and see life clear remains to be seen. Poetry is a jealous goddess and demands singleness of her servants. Some affirm that our Mr. Lowell, our first man of letters as he is, had reached starrier heights save for his laborious years at Harvard and his later life as diplomat and man of the world. None of the younger English poets has written so much as Mr. Noyes, and if you compare his work with that of Tennyson at the same age, you will say that the younger man is not a whit inferior in fancy and feeling and skill, and that the range of his interests and subjects is far wider. Mr. Noyes illustrates the fact that a true poet in the modern world is not a recluse nor a dreamer, but an interpreter because a brother man. He is as human as Browning and with as red blood in his veins. He is what Kipling calls "a man in a world of men." He rowed three years in the Oxford eight; he has a wholesome view of life; he is willing to face all the facts but with an undaunted optimism.

He feels the beauty and hears the music of nature; every scene makes its impress upon him, and he gives it to its faintest touch; but nature has some concord with humanity, it is also a mirror of the soul. It is like a double rainbow, the lower arch distinct in form and color, and then above it, fainter and more wonderful, the bow of promise. This union of nature and man, of the natural and the spiritual, in a lesser poet might descend into flat and stale moralizing, but Mr. Noyes' sincerity and naturalness and his true sense of beauty convey his message with artistic strength. You may open the volumes almost at random to find this truth shining from the page. I choose "Gorse," one among many, for its color and life and its interpretive quality.

Between my face and the warm blue sky
The crisp white clouds go sailing by,
    And the only sound is the sound of your breathing,
The song of a bird and the sea's long sigh.

Here, on the downs, as a tale re-told
The sprays of the gorse are a-blaze with gold,
    As of old, on the sea-washed hills of my boyhood,
Breathing the same sweet scent as of old.

Under a ragged golden spray
The great sea sparkles far away,
    Beautiful, bright, as my heart remembers
Many a dazzle of waves in May.

Long ago as I watched them shine
Under the boughs of fir and pine,
    Here I watch them to-day and wonder,
Here, with my love's hand warm in mine.

The soft wings pass that we used to chase,
Dreams that I dreamed had left not a trace,
    The same, the same, with the bars of crimson
The green-veined white, with its floating grace,

The same to the least bright fleck on their wings!
And I close my eyes, and a lost bird sings,
    And a far sea sighs, and the old sweet fragrance
Wraps me round with the dear dead springs,

Wraps me round with the springs to be
When lovers that think not of you or me
    Laugh, but our eyes will be closed in darkness,
Closed to the sky and the gorse and the sea,

And the same great glory of ragged gold
Once more, once more, as a tale re-told
    Shall whisper their hearts with the same sweet fra-
        grance
And their warm hands cling, as of old, as of old.

Dead and un-born, the same blue skies
Cover us! Love, as I read your eyes,
    Do I not know whose love enfolds us,
As we fold the past in our memories,

Past, present, future, the old and the new?
From the depths of the grave a cry breaks through
    And trembles, a sky-lark blind in the azure,
The depths of the all-enfolding blue.

O, resurrection of folded years
Deep in our hearts, with your smiles and tears,
    Dead and un-born shall not He remember
Who folds our cry in His heart, and hears.
                    (Vol. II, p. 68.)

Mr. Noyes does not stand for any single school of
poetry. There is a touch of Keats and of Swinburne
and even more of Tennyson. He is composite in the
sense that he is a lover of all that is beautiful and true,
a student of the great masters of his art, receiving from
all of them, yet winning his way to his own message

and manner, the waters of a hundred springs running clear and sparkling in his verse. He looks through faëry casements at old romance, but he is not blinded to the romance of common life. He sings the ballads of ancient bravery and love, and he sees the heroic in the men and movements of his own day. He may lack the sturdy realism of Gibson, the optimism that discovers some element of manhood in the hardest lot, but he casts over all life the glamour of fancy and of love. He sings of the "Fisher Girl," and the "Song of the Wooden-legged Fiddler," and the "Barrel Organ," the instrument of the poor, and gives them all music and light.

There's a barrel-organ carolling across a golden street
    In the city as the sun sinks low;
And the music's not immortal; but the world has made it
    ` sweet
    And fulfilled it with the sun-set glow;
And it pulses through the pleasures of the city and the
    pain
That surround the singing organ like a large eternal
    light;
And they've given it a glory and a part to play again
In the symphony that rules the day and night.

Mr. Noyes has the spirit of Sir Henry Newbolt in glorifying the gallant deeds of his countrymen. From the rollicking song of "Forty Singing Seamen" to such noble tributes as "Drake" and "Nelson's Year," he interpreted the adventure and great deeds and mission of England. But he is sensitive to the heroic in common life and sings the victories of peace even more than war, and helps his countrymen to appreciate the men of

thought and duty and creative beauty that have helped
to make the greatness of the race.

> Who are the Empire-builders? They
> Whose desperate arrogance demands
> A self-reflecting power to sway
> A hundred little self-less lands?
>
> Lord God of battles, ere we bow
> To these and to their soulless lust,
> Let fall Thy thunders on us now
> And strike us equal to the dust.

It is impossible, in a brief space, to give the true
impression of the variety and richness of Mr. Noyes'
poetry. The spiritual purpose and light of it is my
chief purpose. Many of the poems deal directly with
religious questions, as "The Old Skeptic," "Christ
Crucified," "De Profundis," and "The Quest." And
where the themes are not distinctly religious, the thought
rises as naturally to a higher theme as the mist into
the upper air.

Mr. Noyes looks at *nature* through spiritual eyes. To
him it is an illumined manuscript of God. The popular
modern doctrine that nature is non-moral cannot suit
him. He never thinks of it as force or law, but a
divine, beneficent life. He reads it as the symbol of
eternity.

But Mr. Noyes goes far beyond a natural theology.
He has the distinctly Christian conception that this is
God's world, and that the meaning and purpose of
human life are only understood in the person of Christ
and his Cross. And here is the source of his optimism.
The man who finds in nature the symbol of the eternal,
who interprets life as the growing of a soul, its pain

and struggle as the discipline for a higher life, does not regard Death as the dread enemy but the messenger of something better to come. The music and beauty, the joy and faith of Alfred Noyes are blended in the "Resurrection."

Once more I hear the everlasting sea
　　Breathing beneath the mountain's fragrant breast,
Come unto Me, come unto Me,
　　And I will give you rest.

We have destroyed the Temple and in three days
　　He hath rebuilt it—all things are made new:
And hark what wild throats pour his praise
　　Beneath the boundless blue.

We plucked down all His altars, cried aloud
　　And gashed ourselves for little gods of clay!
Yon floating cloud was but a cloud,
　　The May no more than May.

We plucked down all His altars, left not one
　　Save where, perchance (and ah, the joy was fleet),
We laid our garlands in the sun
　　At the white Sea-born's feet.

We plucked down all His altars, not to make
　　The small praise greater, but the great praise less,
We sealed all fountains where the soul could slake
　　Its thirst and weariness.

"Love" was too small, too human to be found
　　In that transcendent source whence love was born:
We talked of "forces": heaven was crowned
　　With philosophic thorn.

"Your God is in your image," we cried, but O,
　　'Twas only man's own deepest heart ye gave,
Knowing that He transcended all ye know,
　　While we—we dug His grave.

Denied Him even the crown on our own brow,
   E'en these poor symbols of His loftier reign,
Levelled His Temple with the dust, and now
   He is risen, He is risen again,

Risen, like this resurrection of the year,
   This grand ascension of the choral spring,
Which those harp-crowned heavens bend to hear
   And meet upon the wing.

"He is dead," we cried, and even amid that gloom
   The wintry veil was rent! The new-born day
Showed us the Angel seated in the tomb
   And the stone rolled away.

It is the hour! We challenge heaven above
   Now, to deny our slight ephemeral breath
Joy, anguish, and that everlasting love
   Which triumphs over death.

In great imaginative interpretation of the forces of life, in musical movement that voices the heart's noblest response to it, Alfred Noyes tells us that the noblest poetry is religious, that it makes the music that is helping to build the world.

"Of all the materials for labor," says Lord Dunsany, the Irish poet and playwright, "dreams are the hardest; and the artificer in ideas is the chief of workers, who out of nothing will make a piece of work that may stop a child from crying or lead nations to higher things. For what is it to be a poet? It is to see at a glance the glory of the world, to see beauty in all its forms and manifestations, to feel ugliness like a pain, to resent the wrongs of others as bitterly as one's own, to know mankind as others know single men, to know Nature as botanists know a flower, to be thought a fool, to hear at moments the clear voice of God."

CHAPTER XII

The Poet and the Preacher

CHAPTER XII

"Where are your American Poets?" was the question
Lord Bryce asked of an American audience during the
early days of the war, when he was in this country as
the official representative of Great Britain. It seemed
a strange question to some and they were rather confused by it and others were inclined to laugh. But it
soon appeared that Mr. James Bryce was never more
in earnest and penetrative, and for a day it became the
topic of our chief editorials. Coming from a man recognized by all to be so distinguished in letters and
diplomacy, and a confirmed friend of America, it no
doubt helped to lift our thought for a moment from the
use and worship of things to the real values of life and
the glory of a nation. Mr. Roosevelt in his many-
sidedness and abounding vitality delighted in heralding
a new poet as in discovering a new river. But this is
not the attitude of our workers, our men of affairs or
our men of State. Our workers are too eager to gain
the earth, our scientists and public men too intent on
fact for the quiet of the world of truth and beauty.
Mr. Bryce could ask no more searching and revealing
question: Do we see beyond our little spot of earth?
Do we have imagination to realize the truths we know?
Do we have aspirations for something better, sympathy
for truth and heroism? These are the real treasures

of life.   The great men of our day are not all iron-masters, or multimillionaires, or politicians.   The men who minister to the ideal side of life are our real benefactors.

> Blessings be with them—and eternal praise,
> Who gave us nobler loves, and nobler cares,—
> The Poets, who on earth have made us heirs
> Of truth and pure delight by heavenly lays.
> (Wordsworth, 25th sonnet.)

There would be more humanness in our work and we could make it a work of art if we saw and felt with the poets.   We should have more men of light and leading, if the poets were better loved.

But I speak to men who believe in spiritual realities, who deal with ideal themes and eternal hopes, and no men have greater need of the poets or can find in them greater riches of the Spirit.   I speak of

THE POET AND THE PREACHER

I. The poet is first of all the *realist*.   He sees the outer world of form and color and action, and the inner world of force and thought, of feeling and purpose.   He sees more clearly and feels more profoundly because he is a poet.   His mind is a sensitive plate on which the world of nature and the spirit records its faintest impress.   And he is the true psychologist,—not by analysis and experiment but by imagination and feeling, by putting himself in the place of another, feeling with another, so interpreting a life hidden from the common eye and often from the person himself.   And when the outer and inner world combine, as they do in

our best poets, we have pictures of more than photographic realism, and revelations of life that are con-
vincing and cleansing.

Wordsworth has this realism, of nature herself. He
helps us to see, as some great artist does. To love his
poetry is the finest training of the eye; from the daisy
under the hedgerow to the frowning rocks of the Sim-
plan, from the hare that runs races in her mirth to the
woods decaying never to be decayed. We see the host
of golden daffodils, and we have the inward eye which
is the bliss of solitude.

Tennyson makes no mistake in his birds or his stars,
in some common life like the Northern Farmer, or some
great historic character, like à Becket or Queen Mary.
Is there a more vivid and condensed picture in poetry
than his "Eagle":

> He clasps the crag with crooked hands;
> Close to the sun in lonely lands,
> Ringed with the azure world he stands.
> The wrinkled sea beneath him crawls;
> He watches from his mountain walls,
> And like a thunder-bolt he falls.

And "In Memoriam" has the psychology of sorrow that
is revealing to the most thoughtful life.

And Browning has almost Shakspere's genius in
holding the mirror up to nature, in showing man his
very form and feature. "The Bishop Orders His
Tomb" is the most realistic picture we have of the
Renaissance, of its learning and its selfishness, its
æsthetics and sensuality, its religiosity and its Pagan-
ism; while "By the Fireside" in "James Lee's Wife" as
with a pen of fire lights up the way of two souls in
their growing alienation.

George Frederick Watts, the eminent English artist, painted a portrait of a well-known Englishwoman of society, and she was startled in seeing revelations of the inner life in the eyes, which she thought well hidden in her own heart. And a great poet is the artist of the soul, tracing the thought afar off, revealing the deeper and unknown self, the very secret of the life.

It was the fearless realism of Charles Kingsley that opened the eyes of England to the shameless condition of the farm laborer. In his "Bad Squire" a poacher's widow tells the story:

> A laborer in Christian England,
> Where they cant of a Saviour's name,
> And yet waste men's lives like vermin's
> For a few more brace of game.
>
>   *   *   *   *   *
>
> We quarreled like brutes, and who wonders?
> What self-respect could we keep,
> Worse housed than your hacks and your pointers
> Worse fed than your hogs and your sheep?
>
> Our daughters with base-born babies
> Have wandered away in their shame;
> If your misses had slept, square, where they did,
> Your misses might do the same.

It was big-hearted Tom Hood that made men see the blood on the clothes they wore, the unjust recompense of the poor:

> O men with sisters dear!
> O men with mothers and wives!
> It is not linen you're wearing out,
> But human creatures' lives!

Stitch—stitch—stitch,
In poverty, hunger, and dirt,—
Sewing at once, with a double thread,
A shroud as well as a shirt.

It was the searching eye of Mrs. Browning that saw
that the prosperity of England was being built on a
child's broken body, a fearful mortgage on the future.

They look up with their pale and sunken faces,
    And their look is dread to see,
For they mind you of their angels in high places,
    With eyes turned on Deity;—
"How long," they say, "how long, O cruel nation,
Will you stand, to move the world, on a child's heart,
Stifle down with a mailed heel its palpitation,
And tread onward to your throne amid the mart?
Our blood splashes upward, O gold-heaper,
    And your purple shows your path;
But the child's sob in the silence curses deeper
    Than the strong man in his wrath.

It is said that Steel is King to-day, as Cotton was
with our fathers. It is entering into the varied forms
and uses of industry. It is helping to build the world
to-day. But the world's work is chiefly human, not
coal and iron. And a poet like Mr. Carl Sandburg, who
uses verse so freely that it is hard to distinguish between
prose and verse,—gives us such an impressionist picture of the whole industrial process, both material and
human, that we feel the cost of so-called progress, and
are resolved that it shall not make cheap the souls of
men.

A bar of steel—it is only
Smoke at the heart of it, smoke and the blood of a man.

A runner of fire ran in, ran out, ran somewhere else,
And left—smoke and the blood of a man
And the finished steel, chilled and blue.
So fire runs in, runs out, runs somewhere else again,
And the bar of steel is a gun, a wheel, a nail, a shovel,
A rudder under the sea, a steering gear in the sky;
And always dark in the heart and through it,
Smoke and the blood of a man.
Pittsburg, Youngstown, Gary—they make their steel
    with men.

War may be a dire necessity, "to front a lie in arms
and never yield" may be a test of manhood, and sacrifice
the way of life.   But when the earth is studded with
ten million graves and helpless peoples are crushed
under the wrecks of war: when the bars of the jungle
have been let down and the beastly passions of the race
still cry for blood, it is well for the new generation to
face the terrible realism of Siegfried Sassoon, even
repulsive in its honesty.

The Bishop tells us: "When the boys come back
They will not be the same; for they'll have fought
In a just cause: they lead the last attack
On Antichrist; their comrades' blood has bought
New right to breed an honorable race.
They have challenged death, and dared him face to face."
"We're none of us the same!" the boys reply.
"For George lost both his legs; and Bill's stone blind;
Poor Jim's shot through the lungs and like to die;
And Bert's gone syphilitic; you'll not find
A chap who's served that hasn't found some change."

And the Bishop said: "The ways of God are strange."

If we who are prosperous only knew and could see so as to feel, what burdens and cripples millions of our fellow-men, so numbs or presses the soul out of them, so that they care no more for the great truths that are dear to us than for last year's weather reports, we could not be satisfied with our personal religion and indifferent to the effort to apply the truths of our Gospel to social conditions. If we could visualize a generation of children, ill-fed, anemic, cripples at the threshold of life, peoples broken and scattered, bitter and hopeless, we could not as a nation be content with any Godlike isolation, counting and hoarding our gains, but recognize our kinship with mankind and govern our life by the law of good will to all nations. The same law governs life, national and individual. Selfishness is death. A generous service is life.

The poets are interpreters of life, teach us to see things as they are, not to live in a dream or a lie, but to take our true place and do our true work in the great world of God and nature and human life.

II. The poets are not only realists but *idealists*, not only interpreters of actual life, but of possible life, of those rare moments when the capacity of man awakes and shows its true nobility. This is the very nature of poetry. It deals in beauty, and beauty is not gross and bare but a form of perfection. It deals in music and that means harmony, all parts fitted to their place and work. It deals with life, with its finer aspects and higher motives, and even casts over the baser and more tragic aspects a light that renders them human and remedial.

I know there is a view of poetry that casts away all the reserves of life, that throws open every side of life to the curious and morbid gaze of men, that mocks at all moral distinctions, that calls nothing sacred, nothing profane. It is the lower realism of a pagan revival, the celebration of "I myself," a lawless self-creation, the glorification of all the parts and passions of man as equally to be used and enjoyed.

It may be admitted that in freedom there is progress, that a youthful egotism is better than a slavish conservatism, that the new poetry in its "detective spirit" adds to the understanding of life.

But a lower realism may be a caricature of man. Impression, however vivid, may be only a half truth. You must crown realism with idealism if you are to have the whole truth of man. I lived as a young minister near to the scene of Masters' "Spoon River Anthology." It would be easy in my own town to be cynical over the weakness and foibles of men. But that would be sadly lacking the vision of life that Jesus had, who saw in the corrupt publican a poverty of spirit and hunger for a better life that made him a great disciple, and in a woman of the street a love and devotion that put her on the side of the angels. We all have a Main Street in our town. There is a Main Street on Fifth Avenue as well as Gopher Prairie. But wherever there is a Main Street, there are hearts that feel for others, and acts of neighborly kindness done selflessly, and that connects the country town, however bare and common it may seem, with the city that has the golden streets.

And it is the noblest office of poetry to help us to see this higher realism of life,—this man as he would like to be and can be. And poetry helps us to attain the ideal. Frederick W. Robertson could not get the workingmen of Brighton into his Church, but he could go to them as a brother man and speak in their labor unions. And what did he talk about as a Christian teacher? Why! nothing less impossible than Wordsworth. He knew that if he could break through the crust of habit, lift their thoughts above the dull routine of toil, get them to think of beauty and heroism and sacrifice,—then he had found and awakened the soul. and they would understand and welcome his Gospel, the most wonderful ideal that has ever appeared to man.

Take the most common fact of work to-day, the machine. We live in a machine age. The industrial technique is so highly developed that sometimes the machine seems to be all, and the man nothing. The machine stands for the complex and highly developed modern world. Shall it be like a blind fact that rules us and hurts us, or shall we see in it God's forces and God's laws, a servant for the welfare of the race? Let Kipling tell us in "McAndrew's Hymn."

Romance! those first class passengers they like it very well,
Printed an' bound in little books; but why don't poets tell?
I'm sick of all their quirks an' turns, the loves an' doves
    they dream,—
Lord! send a man like Bobbie Burns to sing the song o'
    steam!
To match wi' Scotia's noblest speech yon orchestra sublime
Whaurto—uplifted like the Just—the tail-rods mark the
    time.
The crank-throws give the double-bass; the feed-pump
    sobs an' heaves,
An' now the main eccentrics start their quarrel on the
    sheaves:
Her time—her own appointed time—the rocking link-head
    bides,

Till—hear that note?—the rod's return whings glimmerin'
    through the guides.
They're all awa! True beat, full power, the clangin'
    chorus goes
Clear to the tunnel where they sit, my purrin' dynamoes.
Interdependence absolute, foreseen, ordained, decreed,
To work, Ye'll note, at any tilt an' every rate o' speed.
Fra skylight-lift to furnace-bars, backed, bolted, braced an'
    stayed,
An' singin' like the Mornin' Stars for joy that they are
    made;
While, out o' touch o' vanity, the sweatin' thrust-block
    says:
"Not unto us the praise, or man,—not unto us the praise!"
Now, a' together, hear them lift their lesson—theirs an'
    mine:
"Law, Orrder, Duty an' Restraint, Obedience, Discipline!"

It is easy to see in the multitudes of new peoples that
have come to our shores, only aliens, the lowering of
our standard of living and bringing us disturbing social questions. We may regard them with bare realism
as the disciples did the crowd coming out of Sychar,
ignorant, superstitious, degraded; a bare and fruitless field: you could expect no good thing from them.
But Jesus saw with truer eyes: he saw the fields white
for the harvest. Like the dull-eyed disciples men think
only of the lower realism;—they speak only of the
Chinaman as a yellow peril or of the dead Indian as
the only good Indian. They speak with scorn and
contempt of the Jew who competes in business, of the
Italian or Slav who bends his back under our burdens,
who digs our sewers and lays our railroads and works
our mines. The poets give us eyes to see better things,
true life behind rough faces and in hard conditions.

They are Idealists and so interpret the real man. I know no better example of this fine idealism, facing the multitudes that strive and struggle here for a footing, than the lines of Robert Haven Schauffler, himself an example of old world strains and new world hopes,—

"SCUM O' THE EARTH"

At the gate of the West I stand,
On the isle where the nations throng.
We call them "Scum o' the Earth":

Stay, are we doing you wrong,
Young fellow from Socrates' land?—
You, like a Hermes so lissome and strong
Fresh from the master Praxiteles' hand?
So you're of Spartan birth?
Descended, perhaps, from one of the band—
Deathless in story and song—
Who combed their long hair at Thermopylæ's pass?
Ah, I forget the straits, alas!
More tragic than theirs, more compassion-worth,
That have doomed you to march in our "immigrant class"
Where you're nothing but "scum o' the earth!"

II

You Pole with the child on your knee,
What dower bring you to the land of the free?
Hark! does she croon
That sad little tune
That Chopin once found on his Polish lea
And mounted in gold for you and for me?
Now a ragged young fiddler answers
In wild Czech melody
That Dvořák took whole from the dancers.
And the heavy faces bloom

In the wonderful Slavic way;
The little, dull eyes, the brows a-gloom,
Suddenly dawn like the day,
While, watching these folk and their mystery,
I forget that they're nothing worth:
That Bohemians, Slovaks, Croatians,
And men of all Slavic nations
Are "polacks"—and "scum o' the earth."

III

Genoese boy of the level brow,
Lad of the lustrous, dreamy eyes
Astare at Manhattan's pinnacles now
In the first, sweet shock of a hushed surprise;
Within your far-rapt seer's eyes
I catch the glow of the wild surmise
That played on the Santa Maria's prow
In that still gray dawn,
Four centuries gone,
When a world from the wave began to rise.
Oh! it is hard to tell what high emprise
In the goal that gleams
When Italy's dreams
Spread wing and sweep into the skies.
Cæsar dreamed him a world ruled well;
Dante dreamed Heaven out of Hell;
Angelo brought us there to dwell;
And you, are you of a different birth?—
You're only a "dago,"—and "scum o' the earth."

IV

Stay, are we doing you wrong
Calling you "scum o' the earth,"
Man of the sorrow-bowed head,
Of the features tender yet strong,—
Man of the eyes full of wisdom and mystery
Mingled with patience and dread?

Have I not known you in history,
Sorrow-bowed head?
Were you the poet-king, worth
Treasures of Ophir unpriced?
Were you the prophet, perchance, whose art
Foretold how the rabble would mock
That shepherd of spirits, erelong,
Who should carry the lambs on his heart
And tenderly feed his flock?
Man, lift that sorrow-bowed head.
Lo! 'tis the face of the Christ!

The vision dies at its birth.
You're merely a butt for our mirth.
You're a "sheeny," and therefore despised
And rejected as "scum o' the earth."

V

Countrymen, bend and invoke
Mercy for us blasphemers,
For that we spat on these marvellous folk,
Nations of darers and dreamers,
Scions of singers and seers,
Our peers, and more than our peers.
"Rabble and refuse," we name them
And "scum o' the earth," to shame them.
Mercy for us of the few, young years,
Of the culture so callow and crude,
Of the hands so grasping and rude,
The lips so ready for sneers
At the sons of our ancient more-than-peers.
Mercy for us who dare despise
Men in whose loin our Homer lies;
Mothers of men who shall bring to us
The glory of Titian, the grandeur of Huss;
Children in whose frail arms shall rest
Prophets and singers and saints of the West.

Newcomers all from the eastern seas,
Help us incarnate dreams like these.
Forget, and forgive, that we did you wrong.
Help us to father a nation, strong
In the comradeship of an equal birth,
In the wealth of the richest bloods of earth.

III.   Then the poet is the *humanist*. I need to call attention to the particular use of the word, not the technical use of salvation by culture, as against salvation by faith, the wisdom of the Greek world and the knowledge of the modern. I use the word humanist in the sense of the Latin poet, "I am a man and nothing of man is foreign to me." And there is no other word to be used for this most significant aspect of the poet.

Of course there are poets who are pets of the drawing-room and of the club, leaders of some exclusive cult, but that's not the breath of true poetry, that blows as free, and universal as our wind over open fields, and through crowded spaces.

All the great poets are universal in their sympathies. They can not build a lordly pleasure-house in which for aye to dwell. They teach the lesson of the lowly cot in the vale. They touch the truths that make men feel the unity of the race; they develop the spirit of true humanity. Dante, a Romanist, places men under one moral government rather than under the laws of the Church. Milton broke from his natural association of Church and Royalist to espouse the cause of man in the Puritan revolution. Byron and Shelley, born aristocrats, were not defenders of class and hereditary privilege, but made song the weapon of human rights. Cowper grasped the unity of human interests. Burns set the hearts of men throbbing with his

> It's coming yet for a' that,
> When man to man, the warld o'er
> Shall brothers be for a' that.

Moore, with pathetic sweetness, voices the sorrow and hope of an oppressed race in

> The harp that once through Tara's halls.

Wordsworth outwardly reacted from the hopes of his republican youth, but in his interest in common scenes and his intimate, loving portraiture of lowly men, he has been a vital force in the democratic movement. Tennyson learned to feel with "men the workers, men my brothers." While the second "Locksley Hall" has not the defiant challenge and hope of the first, the poet has not lost his sympathy or vision:

> Lame and old, and past his time, and passing now into the
>   night;
> Yet I would the rising race were half as eager for the
>   light.

Kingsley and Hood plead the cause of the wronged and weary toilers. Browning reaches the climax of scorn in "The Lost Leader."

> Just for a handful of silver he left us,
> Just for a ribband to stick in his coat,—
> Found the one gift of which fortune bereft us,
> Lost all the others she lets us devote.

His immortal plea for fidelity to the ideal. I heard Dr. John A. Hutton of Glasgow say that three-fourths of the New Testament was written to those who, if they had any sense of shame left, could not be disloyal to any high ideal. Poets have believed in the worth of the essential man, stripped of all the accidents of birth and circumstance, and they have believed in the right of man for the chance to be himself and direct himself and have a voice in whatever concerned human welfare, and the poets have been the constant inspirers of this democratic ideal.

Whatever is truly great in the poets is universal, and we feel in their verse "the touch of nature that makes the whole world kin." Through this universal sympathy the poet is able to see good in men that differ from him, to condemn the wrong without raving at every evil doer of it, to "judge leniently because he can look upon faults as they appear to those who committed them; judge justly, because he can regard the feeling with which he sympathizes from without,—realizing it, but not surrendering to it."

> He who feels contempt
> For any living thing, hath faculties
> That he hath never used; and thought with him
> Is in its infancy.

The poet is a humanist; he puts himself in the place of another, and so he feels the meaning of life, even where his reason questions its faith. A Matthew Arnold can see Messianic entrance into the sin and misery and squalor of East London and exclaim of a devoted minister:

> O human soul! as long as thou canst so
> Set up a mark of everlasting light,
> Above the howling senses' ebb and flow,
> To cheer thee, and to right thee if thou roam—

Not with lost toil thou laborest through the night!
Thou mak'st the heaven thou hop'st indeed thy home.

The poet is the humanist, and he sees the stirring of
the clod, the awakening of manhood in the dull mass,
the age-old contest between darkness and light in the
confused voices and doubtful struggles of human
forces. Edward Markham sees a brother in the "Man
with the Hoe," and he asks the question:

Who made him dead to rapture and despair,
A thing that grieves not and that never hopes,
Stolid and stunned, a brother to the ox?
Who loosened and let down this brutal jaw?
Whose was the hand that slanted back this brow?
Whose breath blew out the light within this brain?
Is this the Thing the Lord God made and gave
To have dominion over sea and land:
To trace the stars and search the heavens for power;
To feel the passion of eternity?

   *   *   *   *   *

O masters, lords and rulers in all lands,
How will the future reckon with this man?
How answer his brute question in that hour
When whirlwinds of rebellion shake the world?
How will it be with kingdoms and with kings,
With those who shaped him to the thing he is,
When this dumb Terror shall reply to God,
After the silence of the centuries?

The poet has such sympathy with men, he so believes in the rights of men, that even in the radical
assertion of these rights through extreme views and
even revolutions, that cause the timid to tremble and
the faithless to think that the foundations are destroyed,
he sees the inevitable harvest of cruelty and oppres-

sion,—the seed of a wider sowing of justice and liberty
and brotherhood.

All the younger poets are democratic in their sympathies, and many of them cry aloud in the passion of
their faith. Even free verse is the expression of their
plea that every fetter should be broken from the spirit
of man.

James Oppenheim declares that to enter the doors of
souls in the hives of the tenement, "swirled in the human
storms" is to "live five lives in the place of one."

> That I may know, beyond grandeur of earth,
>   O man, even here in the pitiful gloom
> Of these shattered walls, God's grandeur sweeps,
>   Yea, in a little room.

And he affirms that

> We builders of cities and civilizations walled away from
>   the sea and the sod
> Must reach, dream-led, for our revelations through one
>   another—as far as God.
> Through one another, through one another, no more the
>   gleam on sea and land,
> But so close that we see the Brother, and understand, and
>   understand!
> Till, drawn in swept crowd closer, closer, we see the gleam
>   in the human clod,
> And clerk and foreman, peddler and grocer are in one
>   Family of God.

IV. And finally, the poet is the *prophet*. The
noblest poets have been conscious that they were not
their own masters, that they were voices of a higher
power than themselves. And critics are not so very
wrong in sometimes seeing in great poems more than the
poets themselves are conscious of writing. "Poet and

Prophet differ greatly in our loose modern notions of them," says Carlyle. "In some old languages the titles are synonymous. *Vates* means both prophet and poet; and indeed at all times, prophet and poet, well understood, have much kindred meaning. Fundamentally, indeed, they are still the same; in this most important respect especially, that they have penetrated both of them into the sacred mystery of the universe. Whoever may forget this divine mystery, as the realized thought of God, the *vates,* whether prophet or poet, has penetrated into it, is a man sent hither to make it more impressively known to us." And Tennyson gives the poet his prophetic place:

> He saw through life and death, through good and ill,
> He saw through his own soul;
> The marvel of the Everlasting Will,
> An open scroll,
> Before him lay.

The poet has been the *foreteller* of the race. And this power to see the future in the instant is not confined to the poet-prophets of the Bible. In this sense there have been prophetic voices among modern English poets. Years before Darwin or Wallace stated the theory of Development, which has so vitally affected every realm of thought and effort, the poets saw life as a whole, and through struggles and changes and growths, man as the crowning purpose of it all. Forty years before the "Origin of Species," Shelley in his "Prometheus" had the dream of an unconscious universe gradually informed with conscious life and love. The last act of Browning's "Paracelsus" is a still clearer prophecy. It taught that

> God dwells in all,
> From life's minute beginnings, up at last
> To man.

But more wonderful still is the word of Tennyson, after years of question and reflection still the poetic interpretation of Development.

> Arise and fly
> The reeling Faun, the sensual feast;
> Move upward, working out the beast,
> And let the ape and tiger die.

This light on the future is not given the poets by magic or special revelation, but through their sensitiveness to the voices of God, their eyes alight to the meaning of life and the increasing purpose of its forces. They are forth-tellers far more than foretellers, the foregleam and foreword of progress, the energy of social and spiritual recreation.

There is a materialistic and Godless evolution. If such long processes come to life in man's being, if he is shaped into form by subtle and complex forces he so dimly understands, what chance of God's thought of him and for the freedom of the Spirit? So thinkers may grow agnostic and the crowd become sensualists. But it is the poet that sees the deeper meaning and foretells the growing sacredness of life, and the finer sense of responsibility.

> A fire-mist and a planet,—
> A crystal and a cell,—
> A jelly-fish and a saurian,
> And caves where the cave-men dwell;

Then a sense of law and beauty,
And a face turned from the clod,—
Some call it Evolution,
And others call it God.

*   *   *   *   *

A picket frozen on duty,—
A mother starved for her brood,—
Socrates drinking the hemlock,
And Jesus on the rood;

And millions who, humble and nameless,
The straight, hard pathway plod,—
Some call it consecration,
And others call it God.
("Each in his own Tongue," Carruth.)

The industrial power of the world is regarded now as the means of all progress—and then—as a brute that "devours children's souls and the hearts of women,"

He takes them and he breaks them, but he gives them
    scanty thought.

We bind tight the force of nature and we laugh ex-ultantly:

Now behold, the good time comes for the weariest and the
    least!
We will use this lusty knave:
No more need for men to slave;
We may rise and look about us and have knowledge ere
    the grave.

But the brute said in his breast, "Till the mills I grind
    have ceased,
The riches shall be dust of dust, dry ashes be the feast!

On the strong and cunning few
Cynic favors I will strew;
I will stuff their maw with overplus until their spirit dies;
From the patient and the low
I will take the joys they know;
They shall hunger after vanities and still an-hungered go.
Madness shall be on the people, ghastly jealousies arise;
Brother's blood shall cry on brother up the dead and
    empty skies."

Shall there be endless contest between those who
have power and those who have only their hands and
their brains? Shall our wealth be built on the tenement
and sweat-shop and child labor? Shall our civilization
forever drag at its chariot wheels the broken bodies and
souls of men?

The poet sees something better than the present
strife and chaos. A new day shall come when the
Brute shall be the servant, not the master of man.

All the desert that he made
He must treble bless with shade,
In primal wastes set precious seed of rapture and of pain;

    *   *   *   *   *

He must give each man his portion, each his pride and
    worthy place;
He must batter down the arrogant and lift the weary face,
On each vile mouth set purity, on each low forehead grace.

Then perhaps at the last day,
They will whistle him away,
Lay a hand upon his muzzle in the face of God, and say,
"Honor, Lord, the thing we tamed!
Let him not be scourged or blamed,
Even through his wrath and fierceness was Thy fierce
    wroth world reclaimed!

Honor, Thou, Thy servants' servant; let Thy justice now
    be shown."
Then the Lord will heed their saying, and the Brute come
    to his own,
'Twixt the Lion and the Eagle, by the armpost of the
    Throne.

(Moody, "The Brute.")

Is man a fighting animal and the dream of peace
impossible because contrary to nature? The march of
the race has been the march of armies, and the strong
have risen over the prostrate forms of the weak. Shall
it be so to the end of the story? Shall each nation seek
its own and worship the God of national love, and
forget the God of the whole earth? Shall we ignore
the lesson of nature and history, of science and religion, and deny the bonds that God has made, and call
the vision of a new Internationalism of justice and co-
operation and brotherhood too good to be true? The
poets of all ages have seen the day afar off, they have
greeted it from afar, they have lived in its light; from
the Hebrew poets who sang of the city without walls,
into which the nations should bring their glory, to the
prophet of our own time who

Dipt into the future, far as human eye could see,
Saw the vision of the world, and all the wonder that
    would be;
Saw the heavens fill with commerce, argosies of magic
    sails,
Pilots of the purple twilight, dropping down with costly
    bales;
Heard the heavens fill with shouting, and there rain'd a
    ghastly dew
From the nations' airy navies grappling in the central blue;

Far along the world-wide whisper of the south wind rush-
    ing warm,
With the standards of the peoples plunging through the
    thunder-storm;
Till the war-drum throbb'd no longer, and the battle-flags
    were furl'd
In the Parliament of man, the Federation of the world.

Every true poet to-day has this hope; he raises it a
banner above the world's din and dust, and calls all
true-hearted to the conquest of Peace.

Dreams are they? But ye cannot stay them,
    Or thrust the dawn back for one hour!
Truth, Love, and Justice, if ye slay them,
    Return with more than earthly power:
Strive, if ye will, to seal the fountains
    That send the Spring through leaf and spray:
Drive back the sun from the Eastern mountains,
    Then—bid this mightier movement stay.

It is the Dawn of Peace! The nations
    From East to West have heard a cry,—
"Through all earth's blood-red generations
    By hate and slaughter climbed thus high,
Here—on this height—still to aspire,
    One only path remains untrod,
One path of love and peace climbs higher!
    Make straight that highway for our God."
               (Noyes, "The Dawn of Peace.")
The Poet—

Presses on before the race,
And sings out of a silent place.
Like faint notes of a forest bird
On heights afar that voice is heard;
And the dim path he breaks to-day
Will some time be a trodden way.

We all need the poets to feed our spirits, to give us eyes and heart and purpose, and no man needs them so much as the preacher. Dr. James Stalker of Aberdeen declares that he knows all the best preachers of Scotland and not one of them but is familiar with the nobler poets of the language.

We need the poets that we may know life, not life in its ordinary, factual sense, but the secret of the heart and the forces that are moulding them. A great modern psychologist reads fiction as the material that gives the keenest insight into the workings of life; and a great poet is the best interpreter for the preacher. He has the imagination that looks into the heart of things and the sympathy that makes the realism human and uplifting. A great poet searches an age to the depth of its consciousness and his interpretations are the very language of the age in the deepest things of the spirit.

We need the poets that we may not lose faith in man or in our message. We must live on the ideal side if we are to be masters of truth and masters of human hearts. We must never sink into a low content for ourselves or for our fellows. We must never say,

> A flower is just a flower, no more.
> Man, bird, beast, are but beast, bird, man,
> Uncinct by dower of dyes
> Which when life's day began
> Round each in glory ran.

The Gospel is the greatest ideal of man, an impossible ideal, too great to be true, too good to be true to the worldly mind. A preacher who loses the ideal is a blind Samson shorn of his strength. "Why do men judge life by its low-water marks of depression," said

the late David Swing to a young minister who was
pessimistic over the social and religious conditions of
their city. "If I lose faith in man one hour in twenty-
four, in the twenty-three hours of faith I will do my
work for man." The poets can read the divine thought
in the lowest life, and in the confusion of moral questions, see where real right doth lie. And the fellowship with the poets is the cleansing and strengthening
of the spiritual sight.

We need the poets that we may have the human
touch, be democratic in our sympathies, not live in an
exclusive world of thought and feeling, but minister
to the whole man and the largest man; that we may
not bow before the idols of the market and the forum,
but stand erect in our own manhood, and reverence and
find the essential man, stripped of all the accidents of
place and possession, and help him find and use his
divine right. The poets by their humanness will help
us be men in a world of men.

We need the poets that we may live with a great
hope before our eyes, that we be not chilled by the cold
indifference of men or dismayed by their cynical pessimism, that we may believe in the victory of the vicarious life, that we may hold fast the promise, "Behold,
I make all things new," and though

> The new age stands as yet
> Half built against the sky,
> Open to every threat
> Of storms that clamor by,

we shall labor on, heartened by the great shout of the
finished work, "Grace, Grace, unto it."

"The smallest break in the eternal order and harmony," says Mr. Alfred Noyes, "is an immeasurable vacuum of the kind that both art and science abhor; for if we admit it, the universe has no meaning. The poet demanding that not a worm shall be cloven in vain, or crying with Blake that a robin in a cage shakes heaven with anger, are at one with that profound truth, a sparrow shall not fall to the ground without our Father's knowledge. The blades of the grass are all numbered. There is no break in the roll of that harmony 'whereto the worlds beat time,' and it is because great art brings out, as a conductor with a wand, the harmonies hidden by the dust of daily affairs, that in poetry, as time goes on, our race will come to find an ever surer and surer stay."

I

Ye that follow the vision
  Of the world's weal afar,
Have ye met with derision
  And the red laugh of war;
Yet the thunder shall not hurt you,
  Nor the battle storms dismay;
Though the sun in heaven desert you,
  "Love will find out the way."

* * * * *

IV

Your dreamers may dream it
  The shadow of a dream,
Your sages may deem it
  A bubble on the stream;
Yet our kingdom draweth nigher
  With each dawn and every day,
Through the earthquake and the fire
  "Love will find out the way."

V

Love will find it, though the nations
  Rise up blind, as of old,
And the new generations
  Wage their warfares of gold;
Though they trample child and mother
  As red clay into the clay,
Where brother wars with brother,
    "Love will find out the way."
                    (Song in "Drake," Noyes.)